AF149557

The Ordinary, the Enchanted and the Quaintly Happy

Sachin Jha is an engineer from IIT Delhi. He runs a chemical manufacturing business in Rajasthan and is an avid reader. This is his second book, the first being *It All Adds Up*.

Also by the Author

It All Adds Up

The Ordinary, the Enchanted and the Quaintly Happy

SACHIN JHA

RUPA

This is a Print On Demand copy and hence does not have special finishing on the cover.

Published by
Rupa Publications India Pvt. Ltd 2017
7/16, Ansari Road, Daryaganj
New Delhi 110002

Sales centres:
Allahabad Bengaluru Chennai
Hyderabad Jaipur Kathmandu
Kolkata Mumbai

Copyright © Sachin Jha 2017

This is a work of fiction. Names, characters, places and incidents are
either the product of the author's imagination or are used fictitiously
and any resemblance to any actual person, living or dead, events or
locales is entirely coincidental.

All rights reserved.
No part of this publication may be reproduced, transmitted,
or stored in a retrieval system, in any form or by any means,
electronic, mechanical, photocopying, recording or otherwise,
without the prior permission of the publisher.

ISBN: 978-81-291-4516-1

Second impression 2017

10 9 8 7 6 5 4 3 2

This book is sold subject to the condition that it shall not, by way of
trade or otherwise, be lent, resold, hired out, or otherwise circulated,
without the publisher's prior consent, in any form of binding or cover
other than that in which it is published.

For my father, like whom, I wish, I could be…

Contents

Part III

Part I

Lost

Thirteen-year-old Raghu Kumar lay listlessly on his dormitory bed, moist eyes blurring his view of the high ceiling. All seemed lost and life offered little to look forward to. He found himself caught between an abyss of emptiness and gusts of misery that were pounding him relentlessly. Soaked in a sweat of self-pity, he waited for sleep to seep in as he tried to push out recollections of the event that had led to this predicament.

Just a couple of hours back, he had lost the pre-quarter finals of the intra-hostel squash tournament.

The ability of putting such setbacks in perspective rarely ever ripens at that age—or for that matter any age. To make matters worse, Raghu's uncle, who also happened to be his local guardian, had come visiting in the evening and in what could be called a display of gross immaturity, had offered advice instead of empathy. He had tried to explain the insignificance of the loss to Raghu by superciliously harping upon the limited bearing hostel squash tournaments have on the overall life of a person. In turn, Raghu had retorted that squash tournaments were no less important than the wish to own a car—which is what his uncle's present fixation was. Uncle had left in a huff and Raghu had duly returned to his sulking.

It's perhaps quite a blessing that most people don't in advance realize the real relevance and worth of the goals which they seek to attain. The world would become an extremely dull and inactive place were that to happen.

And in due accordance with that blessing, to Raghu, what mattered the most now, was the squash tournament. It mattered that despite being one of the better players in his hostel's junior subdivision, he had lost. And it mattered that on-lookers had cheered at his defeat. The cheer, were it to be considered from the viewpoint of an unbiased observer, was merely the kind which often accompanies the victory of an underdog. But Raghu was not unbiased. Moreover, he was a victim, not an observer. He saw the cheer in a totally different light. To him it was an irrefutable confirmation of a belief which he had long harbored; *they* disliked him. Or at best were indifferent to him. Why, even the sparse few he was on amiable terms with had not come up to console him. Abhay Thakur, his only trusted friend, had dismissed the whole affair with a succinct 'better luck next time'. How callous! The least Abhay could have done was to sit down with him, if only in silence. But why would Abhay care! Abhay would have at least two trophies (and that was discounting the 'best in games' for which he had a fifty-fifty chance) to display at the term end. Nobody cared! Raghu remembered when he had acquired his first wristwatch in the second grade and it had received its first scratch even before he could properly tell the time. He'd shown it to Steven who had just as callously remarked 'Nothing lasts forever'. Precocious Steven!

But Abhay had always been okay. Wasn't he the only one who'd stood up for him when, as a fresher, vile insinuations were made about his light-green eyes? Heredities were questioned and the fact that his family was an expatriate in the UK hadn't exactly helped his case. Yes, Abhay was okay. At least he wasn't like the rest of them—that loathsome majority who Raghu could never see eye to eye. Of course, were someone to ask him what exactly it was that made that majority loathsome, he never would have been able to put a finger on it. But that obviously didn't induce him to reassess his opinion; and in accordance with that most mischievous of rationalizations, inadequacy of reason was allowed to be confused with ineffability.

Interestingly, Raghu in fact did have a proper reason to blame the majority's loathsomeness upon. He belonged to a backward caste. This, clearly, was no ordinary alibi. It was a reason potent enough to bear the burden of an entire life's failures. And yet, if that reason hadn't been able to get so much as a foot into the door, it was mainly because a royal snub had dealt with it. Raghu's ecosystems weren't really the type that held caste in high worth. They preferred other candidates for their attention. If UK was preoccupied with race and class, Scads heaped all available consideration on sports and debates.

Also, it was no small help that Raghu had a blend-in-the-background surname like 'Kumar'. This was a middle name common to several castes; and using it as a last name—by truncating the tongue-twisting surname—was common practice for immigrants who lived in a country of different phonetic sensibilities.

Benign Providence had thus duly ensured that *they* end up less loathsome than they had the potential to be.

But still, concluded Raghu, the bottom-line very much lay in what he was reading in the library the other day—Excerpts from the teachings of Buddha. He recollected the part where Buddha exhorts his followers to seek their own path to salvation because no one—not even Buddha himself—could lead them upon it. And in this, it so seemed to the young Raghu, lay the central message of Buddhism and life: every man for himself.

Raghu woke up next morning to find that the more painful memories had faded away. Then, as the rush of a typical boarding-school day absorbed him in its tightly-packed schedule, even the ones that had lingered, slowly disappeared. It was only late in the evening that they could be seen tottering back; and only because they had been summoned by a master who felt guilty that he had not suffered adequately. But overall, the pain had abated, and it was only with a kind of deliberate effort that Raghu could impart to it some of the viciousness which had been there last night.

Sorrow—at least the variety that is of our own creation—is in some ways not too different from an aching tooth. Both have to be continually touched to remind one how much they hurt. And both seek remedy through the same devices: a 'filling' of time garnered memory loss, or, in more severe circumstances, a Freudian procedure of 'root' canal therapy.

Curiously, a timely brushing away of the irritant is seldom resorted to.

Opinion poles

The last period in school was proving to be very taxing indeed. Despite being aware that the teachers were looking to him to complete the Q&A routine—he being reasonably intelligent and eager to please with his quick answers—Raghu was finding it very difficult to pay attention in class. All he could think of was the football match that would start within an hour and a half. This was to be the first time that he would represent his house in an outdoor sport. It was his chance to hunt with the hounds and jog with the jocks; a chance he had long waited for.

Interestingly, the chance had come to him not because of any sudden improvement in his sporting prowess but due to a stroke of luck. Or shall it be said, conjunctivitis. The ailment had taken down three players which led to Raghu's promotion into the team. It was to his credit that he had remembered a similar breakout from the previous rains and had taken due precautions to guard against it. Soap was a fast moving commodity in the Kumar cupboard. And thus the match!

It was an inter-house C-Group game but to Raghu it meant no less than a world cup playout. He had been able to think of nothing else ever since he had been informed of his inclusion into the team. The whole match had been played out in his mind umpteen number of times by then. However, being circumspect even with his fantasies, Raghu hadn't visualized any solo streaks that would result in brilliant goals. All he hoped for was a chance shot into the net that would come by virtue of being in the right place at the right time—something that seldom happened to him. But today had to be different. He knew it.

The school bell sounded... And soon the match whistle went off.

The match turned out to be like any other C-Group game—thoroughly lacking in drama and audience appeal. The ball got tossed around, the kids ran about, foots swivelled and swerved, Maradonian hands of God were brought into play and finally, it happened. One of the kids got lucky with the juxtaposition of his foot and ball, his proximity to the goal post and what had been weighing on the mind of the otherwise bored goalkeeper. A goal was scored. Heisenberg, it is believed, had got the basic material for his uncertainty principle watching one such match. When the ball drifting towards the far-end goalpost had made a sudden swerve and hit him on the face, Heisenberg at once saw the impossibility of simultaneously ascertaining the position and velocity of a particle. But for all his cleverness, Heisenberg could weave into his theory only such uncertainties that pertained to the match. Those which had to do with the aftermath, he didn't dare touch. He steered absolutely clear of the match analysis and post mortem. This was stuff that lay beyond the comprehensible domain of quantum physics.

The analysis involved not only picking the heroes and villains but also rating the also-rans. Scoring against the opponent, or preventing the opponent from doing so, made one a hero. Conversely, missing an easy chance to score, or conceding a goal made one a villain. That was the simple part. The sinister element kicked in with the greys. And since grey happens to be an area of everyone's expertise, every spectator who'd been forced to sit through the match considered himself entitled to an opinion. Also, if that sitting through had been done under the watchful eye of an overzealous senior, which meant the spectators had been obligated to cheer their throats out as proof of house loyalty, the analysis became all the more vicious.

Prejudice, it is said, only deepens under duress.

The general rating procedure went something like this: someone in the crowd picked a player and harped eloquent on his prowess. This of course had little to do with the player's actual antics on the field. It was just an idea, a theory, which the spectator felt was worth propagating. And as it is with most novel ideas, this one too either caught on or died a solitary death. Most times it had to compete with other ideas which arose in other sections of the crowd. Discussions heated up, verbal battles ensued, and thus the fate of many a footballer was decided. Then again, who can say that such is not the judgment criterion for most things in life. In an age of nebulous morals and hazy truths, views and beliefs are allowed to stay unsubstantiated and ambiguous. Indeed, in order to save ideological positions from being categorical, grey has been anointed a primary colour. Intellectuals today no longer need to be faithful to their theories. Their 'insights' are all that they have to hold on to. And in full accordance with this, logic is no longer the tool that chisels out conclusions from facts. The aesthetics of a thought are now more important than its veracity.

Yes, many of these spectator-kids would grow up to be expert commentators on economics, social mores, and of course, politics.

Raghu waited for someone to come up to him and tell him something, anything at all. It didn't happen. He was too much of a non-entity for people to venture an opinion about him. Eventually, he unobtrusively mingled with the crowd and contended himself with a remark or two in the general cacophony.

Not by bread alone

Raghu met Abhay in the evening during their free time before dinner. He had wind of the fact that Abhay had starred in a B-Group match. On other days Raghu would have sat on the sidelines and cheered Abhay but today his own game had kept him from doing so. Better late than never, thought Raghu, and was on the verge of conferring his congratulations when Abhay spoke, 'I heard you played pretty okay today.'

'R-really?' burst out Raghu, 'I mean…yeah…well …'

'Nanda told me about it,' said Abhay, to make up for Raghu's loss of words.

'Oh, Nanda…' muttered Raghu, mentally making a note to definitely attend Nanda's swimming heats scheduled for the day after.

'You can start practicing with the B-Group if you want. I'll talk to Nimit about it.' Nimit was the B-Group captain.

Abhay, who was instinctively aware of the potency of class distinctions, knew that the B-Group manoeuvre was the only way Raghu could hope to play his next C-Group match. He knew, though only at a gut level, of the mind's tendency to categorize people and things into slots of eminence and worth. And he also knew that the only way one could cut loose from an allotted slot was by a quantum jump, and almost never by a gradual inching forward. If Raghu went to B-Group for everyday practice, there was every chance he would blend in despite his below average performance. Once that happened, the reflected aura from practicing with a better group would almost ensure his selection into the lesser group's playing eleven.

Notably, all of this would be made possible by Abhay putting in a good word to Nimit, who, as captain of the team, was not in a position to antagonize his star player. Yes, networking *does* start early in life. And though with time its means keep getting more and more devious, the ends thankfully remain unfalteringly petty.

The remaining walk to the mess hall turned out to be a silent affair. It wasn't in Raghu's nature to get garrulous when inflicted with a favour. His disposition was more towards withdrawing into a cocoon and distancing himself from the spoken word. Who knew which connotation of what sentence would end up offending his holy benefactor! The indebted Raghu even had half a mind to politely decline Abhay's offer but couldn't muster up the strength to do so. Benevolence, they say, is peremptory.

When finally the silence had begun to seem offensive, Raghu spoke up.

'Wednesday. I hope they don't serve up that rotten dal with the pulao.'

Meals were served according to a pre-decided menu. Each day had its specialties and the Wednesday pulao was a much awaited delicacy. But occasionally, the cook exercised his wicked sense of humour by serving a rotten variety of dal to mar the pulao. In such cases, the 'D' in dal could well be equated with the D in the much used acronym KLPD (to the uninitiated, KLPD could broadly be explained as a forced regression from an elated state).

But Raghu was saved the KLPD. The dal, much like his

football match, turned out to be okay. Life was beginning to look up. So much so that even the sight of Chatterji seemed tolerable. Not that Chatterji was some hugely abominable character. But he *did* possess that one fault which Raghu considered to be unforgivable. He was the boy who got to say grace! Then again, Raghu's bias was not totally unjustified. Though grace was said in Sanskrit, Chatterji got to say it because his English was particularly good. For in Scad too, like in most up-market schools, the major criterion for attaining a position of responsibility was a good command over the Queen's language.

'*Twadaymasya Govinda, Twadayamaya Samarpaya.*' Chatterji made no effort to un-anglicize those words of prayer. Raghu had once asked him whether he even understood the import of the grace. Chatterji had not been irked or embarrassed by the question, as Raghu had anticipated. In fact his whole bearing was akin to that of a man answering fun quizzes on a cruise ship. And in keeping with that spirit, Chatterji had casually attempted an intelligent guess, 'Does it mean, look here Govinda, we're gonna have food?' Raghu had smirked. The hiss in his smirk was just about to gather that extra supply of air when he heard everyone laughing. Everyone, including Abhay. They were all laughing at Chatterji's joke. Raghu knew that the so-called joke was absolutely unintentional, and that had further jaundiced his opinion of Chatterji. What everyone had actually laughed at was not Chatterjee's remark but the fact that it was in keeping with his reputation of a blaspheming iconoclast. They had in effect laughed at a string of his previous observations (like the one about Drona and Eklavya from Mahabharata. Chatterjee had wanted to know whether the mere use of a statue was sufficient ground for franchisee claims).

Raghu bravely nodded a smile to Chatterji as he ambled

past him. Chatterji didn't seem to acknowledge it. He was perhaps genuinely pre-occupied and hadn't noticed Raghu's subtle greeting. But obviously, Raghu interpreted the non-acknowledgement as an insult, and that promptly brought his equation with the undeserving grace-sayer back to square one. The euphoria of the football match and the non-rotten dal began to lose their intoxicating effect. Abhay, as if spurred by the awareness of those fading vapours, impulsively accosted Chatterji with a warm hello. The boy responded with equal cordiality and the warmth of the banter that followed went on to stoke a hellfire in Raghu. His was a nasty dilemma—for if standing redundantly in their company was discomfiting, the prospect of leaving without a proper pretext was outright mortifying. Besides, leaving in a huff would be as good as relinquishing Abhay to Chatterji. Raghu ultimately elected to be with them, even as he inwardly blamed Abhay that whole while. He was sure that Abhay had accosted Chatterji on purpose. That was the thing about Abhay, thought Raghu, he always had to stay noncommittal. Every favour he bestowed upon him was invariably followed by something to ruffle things up.

Raghu was partly right. Abhay always *did* ruffle things up whenever their mutual equation took on a mushy hue. This was however a kind of knee-jerk response and not something deliberate, as Raghu thought it to be. Abhay lacked entirely what most males lack in part: the dexterity to handle naked emotions.

As they walked towards their table, from a distance Raghu could spot Shah picking out the choicest pieces of chicken from the serving bowl. He and Abhay would now have to do with whatever was left over, which, knowing Shah, wouldn't be much. Raghu, of course, blamed Chatterji for all this. Even a casual chat with that upstart had to be paid for with a pound of flesh, he was about to say out aloud. But not wanting to take a dig at Chatterji in Abhay's presence, he vented his frustration at Shah instead. 'The early worm gets the bird,' he muttered as they took their seats.

Shortly, the chicken-happy Hasmukh 'pickle' Shah announced, 'I can't wait.'

'Wait for what?' someone asked.

'Wait for the freshers to arrive,' answered Shah.

In the vast plethora of Indian names, where the literal meaning seldom coincides with the disposition of the person, Shah's was an exception. 'Hasmukh' loosely translated into 'smile-face', and Shah's fangs were bared to the world on an almost perpetual basis. The only respite one had from them was when they were dug into some pickle, concocting which was apparently his mother's full-time passion.

'And what's it that you want to do to them Shah?' asked Abhay.

'Well...generally...you know...' faltered Shah.

'Go on.'

'C'mon. You know I'm talking about the ragging session in the common room.'

'But there isn't going to be any ragging. The princi's pretty strict this year. Besides, you heard what Nandy said yesterday.'

Nandy was the kind of senior who could be safely relied to go against any official decree. But this year round, all hope from those quarters had been annulled. Nandy and a few others of his ilk had been made prefects. A rather crafty move by the school administration, thought some. Outlaws (and in-laws) entering politics may not be such a bad thing after all!

'But still, there's going to be some sort of an introduction session,' countered Shah.

'And you're so anxious because you're doing a report on "Nomenclature patterns among affluent Indians"?' queried Abhay.

'Please pass the chapatis,' said Shah curtly, brazenly exposing his inability to meet an argument head-on.

This was what Shah was all about—limited brains and a happy disposition. He found fun in all events and eagerly anticipated them, especially those with which he had nothing to do. One could bet his last rupee that Shah would go through the whole ragging session wearing a grin even wider than the one which he usually sported. The way Shah could soak up all spice from the surroundings, he was quite like those pickles that he was so fond of, and thus gave great credence to the saying 'you are what you eat'.

Abhay was in some ways jealous of Shah's enthusiasm. It was something he had little of. That, however, was not the reason he was confronting Shah right now. The reason was he intrinsically detested ragging, as he detested all such acts which involved picking upon someone smaller than one's own size. He found it exceedingly irksome that someone should anticipate such an act with so much of eagerness.

No, it wasn't a question of ethics. Abhay just didn't find such acts in keeping with his dignity.

The crowd's silver lining

As Shah had anticipated, the ragging session *did* turn out to be entertaining. It had to. The incoming class boasted of a higher than normal percentage of 'locals'.

'Locals' were denizens of the city where the Scad Public School was located. They were people who suffered a plight very similar to that of the Irish in UK, Sikhs in India, and the Pathans in Pakistan; despite having done very little to deserve it, they had a set of jokes dedicated to them.

The reason behind the said injustice against locals was with their numbers. There were always enough locals on campus for fellow scholars to take notice of their typical *patois* and mannerisms. Yet, there were never so many that the locals themselves become the dominant tribe, and thus render fellow students blind to that same *patois* or mannerism. For instance, students from other cities brought along a vernacular twang too; but since students from a single city were never too many, it was difficult to attribute the twang to the city as such. So when somebody from Indore referred to 'snacks' as 'snakes', he could get away without people ribbing him on the nature of the bite. At worst, the elicited rebuke was personal, not aimed at Indore. However, when a local referred to 'rap' as 'rape', the whole of Scad-city had to face the music. Such was the legend of the locals that the word 'local' had ceased to be a noun in Scad. It had become an adjective—and not one with very enviable implications.

The star of the ragging session happened to be a local boy. His name was Abeer Bajwa. Abeer wasn't very proficient in the English language and yet (or maybe even because of it) persisted on using it. From this persistence sprang his gift for Freudian slips.

As the ragging session got underway, the first fresher on the dais turned out to be a lad called Sulabh Kumar. His was an ordinary name, but that did not in any way prevent it from coming under due scrutiny. Apparently, Shah wasn't the only one who harboured an obsession for nomenclature patterns. There were others who shared his fetish. And for good reason, too. In Scad, it was not uncommon to come across guys with famous family names; and then find out that the particular name had been made famous by *their* family!

The moment Ralhan-the-hyena (Nandy's close aide, but neither good nor vicious enough to be a prefect) heard the name Sulabh, he came up with his wisecrack.

'Aha, so you're the guy whose dad runs the chain of toilets.'

Ralhan was referring to the Sulabh Shauchalays. It was a bad joke but Ralhan knew how to extract laughs from an audience. He swerved around with the dexterity of a boxer so as to get face-to-face with the juniors seated behind him. Almost instantaneously, those who happened to make eye contact tittered obligingly. This intermittent wave of titters burgeoned as it fed on Ralhan's resonating chortles. From a very tender age, Ralhan had mastered the art of laughing and talking simultaneously—a very useful attribute for one with an average sense of humour. He showed off his prowess now as he addressed Sulabh amid a guffaw.

'The surprise on your face shows you're not from the Shauchalaya lineage. So what's it that your dad does?'

'Sir, he's a pilot with Indian Airlines.'

'Aha, so he drives a three wheeler!'

This time, the laughs were for real.

This ask-hear-quip-laugh and humiliate schedule was what ragging was all about. Though the freshers had been assured that their non-compliance would not attract any physical harshness from the seniors, it was evident that there was no mutiny on the cards. Fleeting humiliation was a price most were willing to pay for their induction into the mainstream.

But of course, stray exceptions are always there. In this case, the exception was on the dais now—he went by the name of Oberoi. He was a smart Alec from Mumbai whose very informed mother had apprised him of his human rights and entitlements. He was therefore in no mood for being ragged. His whole demeanor was as laid back and informal as that of an American septuagenarian on a Hawaiian vacation. His answers were liberally sprinkled with '*yaar*', 'mate' and 'buddy'. Unfortunately, such were not the preferred nouns by which the seniors at Scad liked to be addressed. Nor did they fancy their fare so raw.

It was a good thing for Oberoi that Nandy-the-Neanderthal was a prefect. Had it not been for the harness of that newfound responsibility, Nandy would have rectified the Oberoi situation instantaneously. But right now, all he could do about the audacious rookie was to mutter a feeble 'next'. With so many freshers around, he couldn't risk Oberoi's going on in that casual tone. He well knew how contagious insolence could be.

'Next' was Abeer Bajwa. Abeer's obsequious body language instantly endeared him to Nandy. So much so that Nandy risked a gambit.

'What do you think of the guy who was here before you?' he asked.

'Frankly sir, I think he was too much of casualty,' replied Abeer. Nandy reflected how close to being a casualty Oberoi had actually come. He wanted to make a remark to that effect but before he could phrase it into the right words, Ralhan ventured into the area of his newfound expertise.

'What does your father do?' he barked at Abeer.

'He's in the railways, sir.'

Ralhan could not immediately come up with a quip. So after a lapse of three seconds—that universally agreed time limit for making a retort—he tried to redeem the situation with 'Oh, a middle-class family!' The words had been uttered with mock scorn. There was no contempt in them, only a desire to arouse some laughs.

'A very middle class family, sir,' replied Abeer with a smile.

'Middle-class by income, or middle class by mentality?'

'A bit of both, sir.'

'By the way,' interrupted Nandy, 'How *do* you define a middle-class family?'

Abeer pondered for a while, as if trying to incorporate the socio-economic aspects of the query into an answer intelligible to all.

'I think sir,' he began 'a middle-class family is one in which at least one member, at one point of time, has emptied one half bottle of hair conditioner, hoping that it would froth.'

There was a short silence followed by a few scattered laughs.

'Froth reminds me,' continued Ralhan, 'What do you think about the sex scandal involving David Pareira and those paparazzi snaps of his wee wee?'

'Snaps of the famous star David and his wee wee? I would

say they were snaps of David and Goliath. How can you call *that* a wee wee?' asked Singhal, another friend of Nandy's.

'You would too, if you were me,' boasted Ralhan, as do most boys that age.

The kind of question Ralhan had asked Abeer was almost routine with newcomers. Scad was no different than most boarding schools. Here too, it was the benevolent seniors who assumed the responsibility of initiating freshers to the birds and bees. They apparently found it extremely amusing to look at coy blushes and to hear answers brewed in half ripe knowledge.

'I asked you a question,' shouted Ralhan 'where are you lost?'

'I'm sorry sir,' replied Abeer. 'Your question just got me thinking whether it is David that kills Goliath, or Goliath that gets David into a soup.'

The laughter this time was more pronounced.

'So, do you think Goliath...I mean David, did it?' urged Ralhan.

'Did what, sir?'

Ralhan was about to explain the 'what' with the choicest of expletives when a quick glance from Nandy checked him.

'Did Mr Pareira commit adultery?' said Ralhan with some satisfaction, surprising even himself with his genteelness.

'I cannot be sure, sir. But since you are insisting on my opinion, I will give it. Facts sir, are pointing that Mr Pereira is adulterated.'

More laughter.

'Adulterated!' spoke Nandy between his laughs. 'Adulterated means impure or tainted.'

'Exactly what I meant, sir,' concluded Abeer.

And so it went.

The so-called ragging session over, Raghu returned to the

dormitory to wind up for the day. He was pleasantly surprised to see that Abeer, who had made a favourable first impression on him, had been allotted a bed next to his. Raghu's first impulse was a desire to assist him with his unpacking. Of course, he didn't actually give in to that impulse. The tacit norms at Scad didn't allow for indiscriminate fraternizing with newcomers. They ordained that 'old boys' maintain a certain degree of superciliousness, if only for the first week or two. And hence, instead of offering a helping hand, Raghu offered a wisecrack.

'So how does it feel? Fingers all greasy trying to butter up the seniors?'

'It wasn't buttering. Actually, we were jamming. Me and the seniors. Two different seeming genres, but making music together for all to enjoy.'

'Music my foot, everyone was laughing at you.'

'And I was laughing with them. Is this not what management gurus call an "everybody happy" situation?'

'Wow! So we're already into management books.'

'And also into books on influencing people, making friends, anger management, happy family life, life after divorce, how to say "cheese" when someone steals your cheese...'

'Pleeeeeese...'

'...basically, books available at the railway station. Father is in the railways, you see. Lot of free passes, lot of travelling. But free passes don't pass time. So one reads on journey. The Chinese say that travel makes man wise. I say that travel which is assisted by these railway platform books will have man wizened in double quick time.'

'Wizened?'

'Yes, wizened,' confirmed Abeer with a somewhat wicked smile before he continued, 'I have an uncle who...'

'You talk too much.'

'That is what spectacle boy said to the football playing black man in *Jerry McGuire*.'

'You *heard* that? I mean, no offence but…you couldn't have deciphered the *firang* accent.'

'I read that.'

'What? *Jerry McGuire* is a book! And please don't tell me it's better than the movie.'

'*Jerry McGuire* is a VCD with subtitles.'

Raghu couldn't help smiling. 'Man, you're something!'

'And what would be name of the somebody who thinks I'm something?'

'That's for me to know and you to find out,' said Raghu with relish. He'd heard that phrase in one of the tackier movies and had been extremely eager to put it to practical use. Having accomplished that longstanding desire, he feigned a yawn and crawled into bed.

Ideally, he would have preferred to continue his conversation with Abeer, but the reason he didn't do so—over and above the constraint of the tacit norms—was that he couldn't risk appearing too sociable. Appearing sociable would have meant that brand Raghu was not moving at a premium in the Scad mart. And since such was indeed the case, he was not totally unjustified in taking the precaution.

But barely had he got into bed when Raghu started to regret his little act of snobbery. Not only had that act brought down the curtains on his nice chat with Abeer, it had also left him thinking whether by being too abrupt he had actually not made a fool of himself. He wondered why he even attempted such games when he was innately so ill-suited for them.('Snobbish pseudos are all right, but you're the only pseudo snob I know,'

Abhay had often laughed at him.).

Raghu peeped from between the sheets and saw that Abeer had opened his second trunk as well. The implication was clear. Abeer intended to finish all his unpacking, even if it meant staying awake till late in the night. This caused Raghu's regret to deepen even further. He knew that late night was the only time one could hope for some respite from the prying eyes of fellow dormitory-mates. And by slipping into bed, he had squandered the prospect of a cozy chat under such ideal conditions.

Ruefully, he racked his brains for a plan to remedy the situation. It didn't take him long to come up with an elementary one.

First, he would get up on the pretext of thirst. Then upon returning from the water cooler, he would casually pick up one of Abeer's things—as if it were an article of interest, then hand it to him to stash in the cupboard...then hand him something else...and thus ease himself into the role of co-unpacker. Perfect.

In keeping with his plan, Raghu got up languorously and proceeded to the water cooler. He sipped half a glass of water and was on his way back to his bed when he was absolutely startled by what he saw. Abhay was standing next to Abeer and the two were having a conversation. What's more, Abhay was smiling—a thing he seldom did. Raghu's plan stood utterly ruined. If he *now* talked to Abeer, it would seem that he was following in the footsteps of Abhay, and that would further bolster his reputation as Abhay's lackey.

It was an untrue allegation—that of being a lackey—but it was something he had had to live with. For alongside the advantages, there is always a price to be paid for the luxury of basking in illustrious company.

Raghu walked towards his bed, fervently groping with the

problem of 'the opening sentence'. Luckily, Abhay spoke first.

'Nimit informs me that you are to practice with the B-Group tomorrow.'

How typical of Abhay, thought Raghu. Never accentuating a favour, and thus making it all the bigger a burden.

'I think I'm okay with group C. My gratitude to *Nimit* anyway,' he replied, giving vent to the kind of irritation that arises when one is not feeling so good about oneself.

'Abeer here is in group B too. You might want to reconsider,' said Abhay in a casual tone. He knew Raghu liked to take a stand and then be adamant about it.

'To B or nor to B, that is the question,' proclaimed Abeer, thus further diffusing the matter. Raghu had to smile and that kind of settled it.

Abhay did not stay long, and Raghu and Abeer were left to chat till late in the night. When they were finally about to call it a day, Raghu asked of Abeer, 'For a guy of your intelligence, did you really have to go ahead with the foolery of ragging?' Abeer thought for a while before he answered, 'How would you feel if you regularly deposited the annual premium to a fund, and when the time to collect the proceeds came, they were denied to you?'

'Of course, cheated,' answered Raghu.

'You see, a few laughs at my expense saved the seniors from feeling that way.'

'And your faulty English act? Was that a deliberate put-on as well?'

'Not entirely. That's an act I enjoy too. As I said, I love everybody-happy situations.'

Games people play

Playing with the B-Group turned out to be a learning experience for Raghu in many ways. To begin with, his football-playing skills improved considerably. But that was pretty much expected. For just as nature strives to do away with vacuums, it also strives to lessen disparities once they become too stark and obvious.

The first two days were rather rough for Raghu. He hardly got to make any contact with the ball. His tried and tested tactic of hanging around in a vicinity and waiting for the laws of probability to do their job didn't quite work in group B. So he learnt to run and to anticipate. He also learnt to adjust to the new ball passing procedure. In group C, that procedure had been considerably different. It consisted in sending out violent pleas to the person in possession of the ball. No one—not even the goalkeeper—was exempt from receiving or emitting such pleas. So rampant were these shouts that in a C-Group football field hoarse throats were more common than sore feet. One would think that amidst such cacophony it was quite impossible for the possessor to decide whom to pass the ball to. But this is where the tacit code came in. According to the code, the possessor always passed the ball to the person whom he was on most affable terms with. Many a friendship had undergone this test of fire and come out unscathed. Others had been suitably sorted out.

In group B, however, the ball was passed in keeping with the requirements of the play. The reason was obvious. Since the players were better, the egos were bigger. The dexterity and shrewdness with which one passed the ball indicated one's competence. Competence in turn went on to build reputation. And who in his right mind would risk reputation over something as fickle as friendship? Who indeed but Abeer. He had a natural flair for the game and could not resist passing the ball to Raghu every now and again. The boy was naïve enough to be guided by his own set of goals; even on a football field!

Abhay, Raghu theorized, deliberately kept the ball away from him for his own good. He didn't want to lay bare Raghu's limited skills. Of course, there was every chance that this rationalization was in fact the truth. But even if it wasn't, Raghu couldn't afford to think otherwise. Abhay was too good a friend to sacrifice to a 'passing' thought. Besides, it's difficult to find fault with people when one is happy. And happy, Raghu definitely was.

Men may father their own limitations but it is society that does its best to nurture those feelings of inadequacy and to bind people to their reputations. These reputations make puppets of people, causing them to act in a given way. And sometimes, the only way to get rid of those debilitating strings is to move on to a different stage. Or a different football group, as the case may be.

The second ballgame that Raghu learnt was how to interact with his seniors. Seniority was a big issue in Scad. Bold and distinct lines were drawn out between boys in different grades. Tradition had it that a senior could be friendly with his junior (if he so condescended) but never friends. And it was on the tricky slopes of such codes of conduct that an individual needed to comport himself.

As of yet, Raghu's interaction with his seniors had been minimal: routine orders from the prefects, a few miscellaneous errands, and perhaps an occasional hello. That was about it. This was the first time he was getting to mingle with them on an informal basis. He was on uncharted territory and Abhay was the obvious choice available for emulation. In keenly observing Abhay, Raghu inadvertently got answers to questions that had long played on his mind. Why, he had often asked himself, did most seniors never employ a tone of irrelevance while talking to Abhay? Why, when four juniors were available at hand and one had to be sent on a trifling errand, was Abhay never picked upon? And why, when addressing him, did they never look through him as they did with the host of cellophane juniors?

Since Raghu's questions were not without their dash of jealousy, he had obviously never referred them to Abhay. The answers therefore came as a doubly pleasant surprise. Abhay, Raghu noted, carried himself with a dignity which was meticulously balanced. He was neither obsequious nor defiant of his seniors; simply polite and to the point. Abhay also took special care to abide by the rules. He fully realized that breaking a rule implied a reprimand, and that if someone were to reprimand and walk over him once, the thoroughfare would automatically be laid open for further use. Prevention was better than cure. Which of course didn't mean that a cure wasn't available! For example, there was the time when Abhay was late for games by a good ten minutes. Nimit had been livid and had asked him to do four rounds of the field. Anybody else in Abhay's place would have pleaded for a reduction in the punishment. Abhay had done nothing of the sort. He had finished his four rounds and had reported to Nimit. Abhay's past record of punctuality had prompted Nimit to inquire the reason for the delay. It came to be known that Abhay had been held back by the housemaster for some work. 'Why didn't you say so earlier? That's a perfectly acceptable reason for being late,' Nimit had remarked. 'You never asked,' had been Abhay's terse reply. Nimit's attitude towards Abhay underwent a sea change after the incident. All for the price of four rounds of a football field!

Be it dear or be it cheap, self-respect always came at a cost, realized Raghu. And since self-respect was a necessary condition—if not a sufficient one—for commanding respect, the respect which he could hope to get from others was always going to be lesser than that which he gave to himself.

Oh, my God!

The small crowd cheered as the gladiators fought.

Gladiator No. 1: Karan Khurana, the foul mouth. And lest this quality be attributed to his parentage, upbringing, or society, it needs to be elucidated that Khurana's foul abusive language was his and his accomplishment alone. He abused because it made him feel grown up. He abused because it made him feel superior. Then when he acquired a reputation for it, he abused because it made him feel identified. But alas, abuses have one thing in common with prayers. They don't always go unanswered. Every once in a while someone would take genuine offence to Khurana's articulations and a brawl would ensue. And even though Khurana was of average height and built, he tended to fare reasonably well in these. Practice, they say, makes perfect. Besides, there were the famous Khurana fangs to be considered; the fangs that provided the expression 'armed to the teeth' with a whole new connotation. In every emergency, Khurana would expertly embed these into the epidermis of the enemy and endeavor to excavate flesh.

What rendered his fangs extra lethal was that they were lodged in such close proximity to his caustic tongue. This was synergy at its very best and there was absolutely no telling which was more noxious—his bark, or his bite.

Gladiator No.2: Varundeep Singh Bhasin, the newly admitted cute Sikh who spoke little and smiled often.

The reason for the fight was the usual one. Khurana had made a remark about the mating habits of Bhasin's mother. It was a run of the mill comment; a figure of speech which was not to be taken literally. But Khurana's emphatic enunciation had once again won the day and the reticent Bhasin had been compelled to reply with fist-cuffs.

Currently, the brawl was tilted a shade in favour of Bhasin. And though this was merely the advantage that is the legacy of the provoked, it managed to sway betting odds in favor of the Sikh. Most spectators began to place their wagers on him. The only ones who abstained from doing so were those who were fully acquainted with the ways of his opponent. No way were they putting their money where they knew Khurana's mouth soon would be.

With the winning odds of each participant so equally poised, the brawl proceeded at a leisurely pace; and it would have continued to do so had it not been for an abrupt interruption. Suddenly, amid the tumbling and wild throwing of arms, Bhasin's turban came off. This was one of those deceptively insignificant freak incidents which are strewn through the course of history and are known to decisively alter it.

The freak incident had no immediate effect on the fighting duo. What actually helped it to gain traction was some valuable input from the crowd.

'The turban has been dislodged! No way is he gonna spare Khurana now,' said one from the horde.

'Oh my God! His religion has been insulted!' added another.

'Khurana is dead meat!' was the conclusion.

Khurana, who was the veteran of many a fight, did not allow such negative public opinion to affect him. Bhasin, however, was more than a little disconcerted. He had already been ruing getting into the scuffle—it being much against his quiet nature—and now this whole thing looked poised to get even uglier. A hunch told him that it was just a matter of time before he would be sucked in even deeper into this whirlpool of the dislodged-turban saga. And yet, he failed to understand why that sentiment of religious indignation had not come to him spontaneously.

Bhasin's lapse of attention did not go unexploited. Khurana, taking advantage of it, landed an absolute stinger on his face. This utterly stunned Bhasin. If he could somehow manage to keep onto his feet, it was only with the support of the bedstead which had thwarted his fall. But soggy knees soon began to take their toll. It was in vain that Bhasin tried to stand upright to the damning authority of pain & rage. Eventually, he gave in, and with a sweeping movement of his arm snatched a hockey stick that had been lying nearby. This was more or less a reflex action. Both Khurana and Bhasin knew that the stick would not be used. It simply wasn't the done thing. It wasn't the done thing because convention—that whimsical despot which usually prefers inertia over logic—allowed biting in brawls but not the swinging of hockey sticks.

Convention would have had its way in the current case too but just as Bhasin was on the verge of putting the stick away, murmurs in the crowd began to get audible.

'Khurana shouldn't have unwrapped the turban,' said the spin doctor.

'You can't do that to a Sikh and get away with it,' added the expert on causal phenomenon.

'Getting personal is one thing, but you can't get at one's

religion,' spoke the moderate voice of secularism.

'Khurana is dead meat!' concluded the budding butcher.

The rush of blood was visible. The otherwise fair Bhasin went absolutely red in the face. Then very deliberately, and with all the strength of the righteousness induced by a fallen turban, he swung the hockey stick. It landed bang on target. Khurana's teeth, which till now had been deprived of all action, finally made their entry into the fray. Two blood spattered ones could be seen lying on the floor and yet another—so it came to be conjectured later—was swallowed up by Khurana.

And thus ended the innocuous little brawl which made Khurana lose his bite for good. As to what Bhasin lost, views could be varied.

Of horse shoes and horse sense

Raghu was superstitious. And though all superstitions are peculiar, Raghu had a knack for harbouring some really curious ones. His current yoke was a fixation for relieving himself in a particular toilet—the last one in an arched row of hostel lavatories. Considering that this toilet was not always unoccupied, and that Raghu often had to wait long minutes before relieving himself, this was a very inconvenient superstition to entertain; not to mention the risk it involved of converting him into what Freud calls an anally repressed personality. But Raghu braved it all stoically.

Raghu, however, hadn't picked up his current superstition solely on a whim. There was some interesting history behind it. Geography too. In the semester that had gone by, Raghu had fared exceptionally well in both these exams. And coincidentally, he had on the days of these exams relieved himself in the said toilet—the last one in the row. The omen was obvious and it had taken little time for the astute Raghu to put two and number two together. He at once saw the toilet for what it was—a slot machine that took muck and gave luck. Ever since, he had faithfully patronized the spot.

Raghu's innocuous practice could have continued unabated into perpetuity. But all good things come to an end. And the end in this case was wrought by a pair of prying eyes that belonged to, who else but, Hasmukh Shah.

When Shah observed—obviously, on more occasions than one—that irrespective of all urgency Raghu always waited for the last toilet to be vacated, he straight away knew that there was something fishy. However, no amount of brain racking yielded an answer as to what exactly it was; and the mystery behind Raghu's chamber of secrets looked well poised to forever remain just that—a mystery. Finally, Shah was forced to invoke his formidable last resort—'the technique'. 'The technique' was a weapon which Shah employed for the dual purpose of garnering popularity (though that of a short-lived nature) and ferreting out information. Once in a summer camp, Shah had effectively used 'the technique' to enlist some eleven best friends for himself. The procedure was simple. Shah would appraise his prey and accordingly concoct a 'family secret' to confide to him. Say, if someone was touchy about his slightly flirtatious sister, Shah would divulge to him that his own sister was in fact a nymphomaniac. And to someone whose mother was not fluent in English, Shah would reluctantly reveal that the woman who bore him had never gone to school after grade four.

These so-called secrets invariably masqueraded as emblems of intimacy and had the victims eating out of Shah's hands.

Raghu fell for the ploy too. When told about the benefits that Shah's mother had reaped from certain superstitious practices, he gushed out the secret of his own harvest.

Shah—ever the gentleman—didn't blow the whistle on Raghu straight-away. He chose to keep the secret with himself. Then one day when he wasn't feeling so agreeable about life in general, he decided to let it go. The venue he picked was the dining table (ample audience, and seated too.) It allowed Shah the leisure of bringing up the topic in what he thought was a delicate manner.

'All toilets are equal, but some toilets are more equal,' began Shah.

There was no response from the audience, but that of course didn't bother Shah. Not being the type who needed cues to explain their cryptic remarks, he continued, 'Our friend Raghu has been hiding something from us.'

Raghu instantly went red in the face. Abhay was quick to notice it and right away came to his aid. 'Why don't you just shut up Shah,' he snapped, 'The food is unpalatable even without your allegories.'

Shah let that go unheard. It was not every day that he got to unleash firsthand mill fodder, masala, as it was called in Scad jargon. He cheerily continued, 'Mirror mirror on the wall, which is the best shit-pot of them all? If any of us were to ask this question to a mirror, the mirror would not answer. But apparently, when Raghu asks this same question to ...'

'Hasmukh,' Shah was cut short by Abeer, 'when you pose your very interesting query to the mirror, I'm sure the mirror reflects upon it. And I'm also sure that by way of answer, it does come up with a reflection.'

There was laughter all around. But Shah was not giving up so easily. He asked the person seated next to him to pass the rice, and thus bought time for the laughter to subside. He had realized that his literary preambles were proving to be no good. So this time, he approached the topic in a more direct manner. 'Raghu was late for morning prep two days back. He could've been on time had he not insisted on using the last toilet. And yesterday he almost soiled his pants but didn't use the vacant pot nearby. What is it with the last pot in the row I ask?'

There was a short bewildered hush before Abeer answered, 'Perhaps, it is the pot at the end of the drain-bow.'

Everyone laughed, and what followed were more lame jokes on Shah. Taking his cue from drains, Gupta, the aspiring humorist, wanted to know 'why the spectacle of a defecating Shah could not be referred to as brain drain?' The next pot-shot came from Dhanker, the macho from Haryana who considered traits such as pickle-nibbling and gossiping to be outright effeminate. A hungry Dhanker had been patiently awaiting his turn at the chicken curry when the ongoing spectacle—that of Shah leisurely rummaging through the bowl for a good five minutes—caused him to snap 'Search on, and you'll find yourself a Y chromosome in that bowl.'

Once again there was laughter all around, and all of it at Shah's expense. Raghu was saved the embarrassment. For just as a greater misfortune has a way of pushing the lesser one out of cognition, the bigger story is often able to attract *all* public attention away from the lesser one.

No sooner had Raghu walked out of the mess hall than he rushed to catch up with Abeer. But for all his haste, it was only after a long drawn-out silence that he could finally utter a word of thanks.

'No problem,' replied Abeer graciously. Then after a short while, he added 'Can I ask you a question?'

'Sure,' replied Raghu.

'What's it like to be ordered about by your superstitions? I know the toilet thing isn't the only one.'

'You don't understand. I come from a very religious family.'

'So do I. But what has religion got to do with superstition?' asked Abeer.

Raghu thought the question to be strange but nevertheless

attempted an answer. 'Hell, everything! Try visiting a temple with my family. It's worse than following a bloody algorithm. The rituals have to be observed like clockwork and one slight deviation is all it takes to blow mom's top off. I mean, even the wrong number of incense sticks is enough to disturb her. Or, if the sweetmeat shop doesn't have the particular *prasad* she had pre-decided upon, she takes it to be a bad omen. And God forbid that the flowers on sale should not be fresh!

'Much as I try not to agree with her but the superstitions keep rubbing off. The truth is that a part of me is now scared of temples. I'm kind of convinced that at least one of my manoeuvres will be out of sync with the required ritual. Would you believe it, I'm comfortable in a temple only when I'm on belligerent terms with God. When the going is good, I view life as a precariously placed house of cards that can be brought down by the slightest disturbance. I have lucky socks, a lucky pen, and even a lucky underwear. There was a time when I was into lucky soaps. But the sparing use interfered with my hygiene and I let go that habit.'

Abeer laughed openly. A half-suppressed snigger would have reeked of dishonesty. Raghu smiled too. He was already feeling better—there being a big difference between letting out a secret and unburdening oneself.

'I think you should meet my father. But till you don't, I could repeat for you some of the things he says,' offered Abeer.

Raghu nodded, urging him to go on.

'Consider the Earth,' began Abeer. 'Even with its billions of humans, millions of species, and all its complex forces, it is after all just one small planet in a solar system. There are millions of such systems in our galaxy, and there are billions of galaxies like ours. Also...'

'Okay, I get it,' interrupted the impatient Raghu, 'You're trying to tell me about the insignificance of our existence.'

'But that's not all,' continued Abeer, 'I'm also trying to tell you about the limitlessness of the show that is the universe, so that you may realize how busy the gentleman running this show must be. Now, don't you think it's quite unlikely that such a gentleman would be bothered about how many incense sticks you burn at his altar? And that it's all the more unlikely that he would turn vindictive upon seeing the wrong number?

'See, it's as simple as this. You can either believe in an absurd universe where everything happens at random, or you can believe in one that runs in order and harmony. If you are an existentialist who chooses the former, there obviously is no reason for you to be superstitious. And should you choose to believe in the latter, you would do well to realize that the laws which keep this vast universe in harmony are, to say the least, intelligent. If you yearn for success, these laws would require you to slog your ass off. Not wrap it up in your lucky underwear.

'And lest you make light of that universal order and harmony, let me tell you that there are people—my father being one of them—for whom that harmony holds the key to everything. In fact, for them that harmony *is* God. A Spinozan God who has neither a personality, nor consciousness, nor will. And nor does that God concern himself with the everyday fates and fortunes of his creatures.'

'Spinozan God?'

'A notion not much different from the Vedantic concept of Brahman. Father says that the reason we don't have temples of Brahma is that it was deliberately intended to keep him faceless and devoid of personality. The wise seers did not want us to confuse Brahma with the white bearded gentleman.'

'And what if I don't want to believe in such a God—a God who's devoid of personality?'

'Then by all means go ahead and choose a God *with* personality. But just be mindful of one thing. While deciding upon that personality, take care not to ascribe your God with attributes that are unbecoming even in a half-decent human being. Attributes such as pettiness.'

'Who in his right mind would ascribe pettiness to God?'

'You for one! Because if you didn't really consider your God as petty, you wouldn't expect him to hold grudges against you for lack of superficial ritual. Or be pleased by your indulging in it.'

Raghu didn't reply.

'Man! You're one precocious bastard,' said a voice from behind them. It was Ralhan. He had been listening to their conversation.

'You may say so,' replied Abeer respectfully, 'but if all this wasn't comprehensible for a thirteen year old, I'm sure my father wouldn't have told it to me.'

Ralhan just shook his head and walked past them. When he had moved ahead a few paces, the conversation stirred again. 'Let me give you a real life example,' began Abeer, 'Father has the sole responsibility of running his office. He has these two clerks who help him out with it. One of them is the standard sycophant with a tongue dripping with honey. Though mind you, he's not at all bad at his work. And on the other hand we have this shy taciturn who's extremely efficient. The man works away at his table, rarely raising his head even to greet father. Now let's assume that father's office was to go on a retrenchment spree. Can you guess which of these two clerks my father would oust?'

'Obviously, the sycophant.'

'If it is obvious to you, it must be a lot more obvious to a person who's running the universe. So you see, it's not without reason that my father says "superstition is the biggest blasphemy."'

'You do seem to have a point,' said Raghu after a prolonged silence. 'Tell you what, today may go down as a red letter day in my life.'

'Too bad you couldn't honour it by wearing your lucky underwear. I think you were saving it for the Sanskrit test tomorrow.'

Raghu blushed, for such was indeed the case.

Special theory of integrity

Despite being deprived of Raghu's lucky underwear, the Sanskrit test wasn't entirely uneventful. Jagira, the invigilator, caught Shah using a *chiththa*.

Chiththas were data transfer devices. More specifically, they were pieces of paper that contained written information pertinent to the exam at hand. Quite in the fashion of money, the essence of *chiththas* lay not in the volume one possessed but in what one did with that volume. There hence abounded various schools of thought on *chiththa* handling. And though all such schools promised to deliver the earnest seeker to the same end, the means which each school employed were different. There existed two main points of deviation. One, how and when an individual executed the 'copy' operation. And two, in the event of distress, which was the orifice he chose for the disposal of evidence. It was plainly evident that Shah had botched-up on both counts.

Notably, Shah wasn't the only one who had used a *chiththa*. He was the only one who had been *caught* using it. This specific set of circumstances subjected him to the theory of common transgressions. According to this subcontinent-specific theory, fairly prevalent offenses—like bribery or infidelity—are deemed by the public to be no offenses at all. They metamorphose into offences only if they chance to fall into the glare of the media or an agency of law. Indeed, till such an expose happens, the dominant emotion which such offences incite in the general public is that of envy. It may be explicit envy, secretive envy, or subconscious envy, but envy undoubtedly it is. For were it not envy, the perpetrators of common transgressions wouldn't be leading such proud and opulent lives.

Yet one single trigger—the perpetrator's indictment—is all it takes for emotions on both sides of the fence to transform. That indictment effects an instant U-turn. Pride immediately turns into a sense of shame. Also, the envy that the public hitherto harboured is straight away transformed into a feeling of ire and disdain. It is as if the public didn't have an inkling of the offender's misdeeds all along; so when confronted with the newly unveiled delinquent, it is forced to sprout moral righteousness.

The public turned against Shah too. He was relegated to being a pariah for about a week, the approximate span of public memory in such matters.

Lunch that day turned out to be a quiet affair. The few feeble attempts which Shah made at conversation were duly nipped and disposed off. To Abeer, all this seemed very unfair. He felt that in a scenario where at least one-quarter of the boys had used a *chiththa* at some point in their lives, the act of being caught was simply a matter of coincidence, and it could in no way be the sole segregating factor between sinner and saint. In truth, Shah's getting caught was nothing more than that—the coincidence of having Jagira for an invigilator.

Jagira was your run-of-the-mill-below-average teacher who having realized that his teaching acumen would never win him any deference from students, sought to draw it out of them through alternate devices. One such device was the raw power that came with the role of an invigilator. Jagira simply revelled in that role. Unlike his colleagues, not once did he complain about vigil-keeping being a dull and monotonous task. In reality, he never *allowed* that task to be dull or monotonous. Where other invigilators merely waited for opportunity, the proactive Jagira went ahead and created it. It was therefore never enough for him that a student did not cheat. The concern that gnawed at his innards was whether the student *wanted* to cheat. And in order to seek the answers to such questions—in order to ascertain that his students were truly honest and weren't merely riding what philosophers term as moral luck—Jagira would lull his prey into complacency by feigning sleep, by being engrossed in a book, or even by totally disappearing from the examination hall. Those who considered themselves smarter than they actually were, usually took the bait. Shah too had paid for such a misconception.

Abeer earnestly wanted to do something to ease the atmosphere but no amount of brain racking seemed to yield a way. Then all of a sudden, it came to him—an inspiration from his railway reading. Abeer waited for the conversational river to come flowing near his pool of thought, and once the two were close enough, he dug-up a connecting canal with a 'that reminds me.'

'That reminds me of the time,' began Abeer 'when an acquaintance of Einstein asked him for his phone number.'

'I'm sure lots of people must have asked Einstein for his number,' ventured Gupta.

'Yes, but guess what was Einstein's response.' No guesses were forthcoming and Abeer continued 'Einstein walked up to the telephone directory, looked up his name, and told the acquaintance his number.'

'Bullshit.'

'The acquaintance's reaction was somewhat similar to that,'

went on Abeer, "'Can't you remember your own telephone number?" he asked Einstein. The boss's reply was calm and casual "I don't clutter my mind with information that can be gathered from another place."'

Abhay was the first to smile. The others took a while to see through Abeer's story. And soon all eyes were on the newly christened Einstein. Not accusing eyes, but eyes somewhat benign. Shah smiled for the first time that afternoon. He in fact went a step further and unscrewed his yet unopened jar of pickles. Abeer breathed an inaudible sigh of relief, for *that* was a sure sign that things were back to normal.

General theory

'You gave away your brand new Levi's to RP?' demanded Raghu of Abeer.

RP was the effeminate *dhobi* who believed in the dictum that if you want something, you ask for it. So asking he did in plenty. Also, RP was shrewdly aware of the fact that when it came to favourable responses, new admissions offered a better success rate. The art of saying no always took some time to master.

'Yes,' said Abeer 'RP has been pleasing me every evening for the past week.'

Raghu's eyes popped out and were on the verge of being sucked in by the vacuum his open mouth had created.

'Oh no, no,' Abeer was quick to amend, 'It's not what you are thinking.' In an all-boys' school, it was easy for a remark to gather a completely different connotation.

'Then please explain "pleasing" to me.'

'When someone says please to you, he is pleasing you,' smiled Abeer mischievously.

Raghu was stymied by not being able to pick a hole in that. He went back to his old refrain 'But tell me, why'd you give your brand new pair of Levi's to RP?'

Knowing that there was no getting away from the query, Abeer finally answered, 'You see, the old clothes that the boys give RP will always be better that the new ones he can afford. So it is highly unlikely that RP will ever buy any new clothes. And this way, he will go through his entire life-cycle without ever wearing anything that has previously not undergone a few wash-cycles.'

'But you really liked that Levi's.'

'Which is why it took me a full week of pleasing to decide.'

'And you aren't regretting it?'

'Not at all. Father says that giving is similar to taking a bath on a cold winter morning. There is an initial reluctance, but once done, you always feel wonderful.'

'Does your father also read a lot of those railway platform books?'

Abeer didn't answer. For once, he seemed a bit offended. Raghu was pleased to discover that there *were* matters which Abeer didn't laugh off. Were it anybody else, he would have saved this knowledge as ammunition for future use. With Abeer, he secretly vowed never to tread that ground again.

The awkward silence that ensued was broken by Shah. He had run in to deliver some news.

'Abeer, your dad's come to pick you up for the weekend. Raghu's been allowed to go along too,' reported Shah with what seemed like a touch of disappointment. Shah had quite taken to Abeer after the Einstein episode. Also, he hadn't been able to do away with hoping for a reciprocity of the sentiment. He had therefore hoped, though not really expected, to be invited for the weekend at Abeer's.

It took about fifteen minutes for Abeer and Raghu to pack their bags and report to the visitor's lounge. Here, Raghu finally got to meet Abeer's dad. Of slight built and benevolent smile, Abeer's father seemed much like the composed and tranquil person that Raghu had imagined. Abeer's mother was different. Being a Punjabi she preferred to keep her attire loud and emotions louder. Barely had she set her eyes on Abeer when the joy of meeting her son poured out in the form of tears and wails. And since these cascades and sound effects were appropriately synchronized, they furnished her with the distinct air of a musical fountain.

Most students in the vicinity scurried to make a quick exit. Some were too embarrassed, others wanted to report the scene to their friends ASAP. The few who stayed behind were the truly sadistic ones. They would leave only after the show was over.

Raghu, who had been getting pinker by the minute, was now a light shade of scarlet. He was going to spend the weekend with the Bajwas and felt partly responsible for their histrionics. In contrast, neither Abeer nor his father showed any signs of discomfort. They patiently waited for the turbulence to subside. Little was said to comfort the lady—nor did the tide of her outpourings provide for any such chance.

It was a good twenty minutes before the party finally settled in the car and the homeward journey began. As was expected, the conversational ball was monopolized by Abeer's mother. The first thing she wanted to know on an urgent basis was whether her son was being served all meals on time (the story goes that if Laxman from the Ramayana was a Punjabi, then the response he would have elicited from his newly-wed wife after suddenly springing upon her the news of his fourteen-year exile would have been *'roti toh khake jao.'* Do have your meal before you leave.) Once her fears about a starving son were assuaged, Mrs Bajwa voiced her next concern: Butter. Was enough of it being doled out with each meal? When told that butter was kept confined to the bread at breakfast, she was absolutely aghast. Her immediate reaction was to accuse the school authorities of misappropriation of funds. Then once that impulsive allegation was dismissed and the affair had been thought over more thoroughly, deeper issues emerged. Mrs Bajwa wondered aloud whether 'all round development'—the supposed reason for sending their son to a boarding school—was an objective worthy of the butter sacrifice.

As Mr Bajwa passed a cursory glance over his wife's portly frame, the obvious connection between butter and all-round development leaped to his mind. He could not keep the giveaway smile in check. But Mrs Bajwa carried on her prattle with unabated enthusiasm.

Raghu, deprived of all attention, was preoccupied with his own thoughts. He was thinking about Abhay with a cartload of guilt. This was the first time since his joining school that he and Abhay would not be spending the weekend together. But more than that anticipated absence, what bothered Raghu was the reason that had led to it.

As soon as talk of the weekend outing had come up, Abeer had extended an invitation to both him and Abhay. Only, Abhay had refused. He had probably foreseen that the housemaster wouldn't allow more than one guest to Abeer's father. What he had also foreseen was that such a last minute refusal would necessitate a difficult decision. Someone would be required to stay back. But who? Abhay? Raghu? Or both? Sadistically, all solutions to the deadlock entailed the singling out of one person—a singling out that could very well leave a small yet ugly mark on their friendship.

Raghu too had anticipated the impasse but hadn't been able to muster up generosity like Abhay's and decline Abeer's offer; and the reason he hadn't been able to do so was because of a purely selfish motive. Raghu, in all his years at Scad, hadn't been able to befriend anybody save Abhay. And there too the bond that existed between them wasn't a mutually dependent or mutually contained one. Abhay could get along with anybody he condescended to. Consequently, he was always there *for* Raghu but hardly ever there *with* him. Theirs was a friendship kept in check by the glass ceiling of respect that one party held for the other.

With Abeer, however, it was a friendship of equals. And it was to build on this promise that Raghu was so eager to visit Abeer's home. Then again, by his own sense of logic, befriending Abeer implied betraying Abhay. It was almost as if he mistook friendship for monogamy.

The problem perhaps lay in Raghu's using his own emotions as basis. Just because he felt a tinge of jealousy whenever he saw Abhay getting overtly friendly with others, he assumed that Abhay too would feel the same. He was obviously unaware that the 'do unto others as you would have them do unto you' principle of reciprocity, when applied, had to be done so with a condition: all other things equal. Raghu's significance in Abhay's life was not quite the same as Abhay's significance in his. Applying reciprocity here was like expecting an equally expensive return gift from a friend who was far poorer. But since Raghu was in no position to appreciate that nuance, he now dutifully engrossed himself with his eight-cylinder guilt engine.

He'd just finished ferreting out in his mind some of Abhay's favours from the past when he heard his name being called.

'Dad's talking to you,' nudged Abeer

'Uhh...sorry. I think I dozed off,' apologized Raghu.

'Dozing off is nothing to be sorry about,' said Abeer's father 'unless you're in the habit of feeling guilty after every luxury availed.'

Raghu couldn't think of what to say and filled up the awkward silence with 'Are we close to home?'

'Quite,' said Abeer, 'just around that next crossing.'

Raghu looked out towards the crossing and was surprised to see the place abuzz with about a hundred men. There seemed to be a commotion at the crossroads.

'What's up?' he asked, gesturing towards the men.

'Oh them,' answered Abeer 'They are daily wage laborers. That crossroad's where they gather to be picked up from.'

Their car soon reached the turn for Abeer's house but could not straight-away be driven into that lane. Too many men were milling about on the road and it took them a good fifteen minutes to make the turn. That, however, was still not the end of their traffic travails. Standing right in middle of the 'home' lane were two men engrossed in conversation—a conversation so gripping that it rendered a twelve foot car absolutely invisible to them. Ultimately, Mr Bajwa had to gently honk. This caused one of the men to turn around and examine what it was that demanded his attention. Seeing that it was only a car, he casually went back to his tête-à-tête. Then after about two minutes, when he turned to spit out the tobacco he had been chewing, the car caught his attention once again. This time he relented. He vacated the road for the car to pass and even bestowed a condescending smile to its passengers. Mr Bajwa smiled in return. Raghu thought the response to be an unusual one but he was too sleepy to say anything. Vaguely, he listened to the ongoing conversation between Abeer and his father.

Soon, they were home. Raghu managed to catch a moment with Abeer while they were getting out of the car.

'Does he always talk to you like this?' he whispered.

'Does who talk to me like what?'

'Does your dad always talk to you like he's talking to an adult?'

'Yes, most times,' said Abeer after thinking about it for a few seconds.

'And he's been talking to you like this since you were a kid?'

'I think not. Only since he read *To Kill a Mockingbird*,' laughed Abeer.

Raghu found Abeer's house to be modest, tidy and unpretentious. But this was hardly surprising as it was in keeping with the character of the habitants. What *did* surprise him was the candour with which the family members addressed each other. No topic of discussion was taboo at the Bajwa dining table—be it the amount of money that was to go into the gift-envelope at a friend's daughter's wedding, or the maid who had pilfered the twenty-rupee note lying on the bookshelf. It simply didn't seem to bother the Bajwas that the outsider could perceive them as petty.

Only two kinds of people could do their dirty linen in public like this, reflected Raghu. Those who were socially unconcerned, and those who knew for a fact that there was nothing repugnant about their linen. He still needed to figure out which category the Bajwas belonged to.

As of now, Abeer's mother was quoting the neighbourhood on the corrupt practices of the newly elected corporator from their area.

'He seemed the epitome of honesty before he was elected. Used to flare up at the mere mention of corruption,' she remarked.

'Perhaps he actually *was* that way then,' observed Mr Bajwa.

'Then how come he changed?'

'He didn't change. His election just unlocked the latent corrupt part of him. Quite in keeping with the Charlie Chaplin dictum.'

'Charlie Chaplin?' asked the boys in unison.

'Yes, Charlie Chaplin,' continued Mr Bajwa. 'Chaplin said that when a man slips on a banana peel, we laugh. Not because there is something inherently funny about the situation; we laugh because it is not us.

'Likewise, when people read or hear about an act of corruption, they express anger. Not because of the presence of some strong moral fibre but because...'

'Because it's not them?' asked Abeer in disbelief, cutting his dad short.

'Precisely. They may not be aware of it but the real reason they're upset is because *they* didn't get that chance. I mean, how else do you explain one lot of compromised office-bearers after another?'

'I don't get it,' said Abeer. 'In the morning you were asking me to be compassionate; to be more understanding of the plight of others. And now you say that most people are congenitally corrupt.'

'Well first of all, I'm not saying that most people are congenitally corrupt. All I'm trying to convey is that most people are extremely vulnerable to temptation. And secondly, what I'm telling you now is in perfect keeping with what I told you in the morning. Once we realize that most people—us included—are vulnerable to temptation, we become more tolerant of those who succumb to it.

'We call ourselves honest. But if truth be told, how many chances of dishonesty have we shut the door upon? When the shopkeeper hands us an extra fifty-rupee note while counting out the change, we promptly return it. When we see somebody's wallet fall out of his pocket, we do the same. And there! We're honest. We're honest because that's the *intelligent* thing to do. Honesty for grabs at Rupees fifty! Hell, the feel-good itself is worth much more than that, let alone the incident's anecdotal value, or the credit entry in the virtue ledger. Only a fool would miss that offer. But the question is, what happens when the stakes are upped?'

None of the boys ventured a reply.

'Well let's for the sake of example concoct a situation,' urged Mr Bajwa, 'Imagine yourself at a desolate railway station. It's the middle of the night and the only soul in sight is the man seated next to you. Then as his train arrives, he too makes an exit. But hardly has his train left the platform when you notice a small pouch lying on the spot where he was seated. Ridden with boredom and curiosity as you are, you end up opening the pouch. And the pouch contains a handful of diamonds. Now, what do you do? Hand over the stuff to the authorities with a description of the owner, or melt away into the night with the packet?'

The silence that followed was once again broken by Mr Bajwa.

'Now irrespective of what you would've done, you've already committed half the crime. You've pondered upon your decision. That's a giant step forward from the knee jerk reaction of returning the fifty rupees!'

The boys squirmed, but Mr Bajwa pretended not to notice. He continued, 'You see, each one of us has a level at which we succumb to temptation. There is always a melting point. Somebody will succumb to x, somebody to 10x. Yet somebody may not find a 100x of interest but will readily give in to y. And then there is the element of circumstance—under different circumstances our reactions to the same temptation are different.

'And therefore, somebody's succumbing to a temptation which *we* would have withstood—or think we would have withstood—does not really give us the right to be judgmental of that person.'

'Are you trying to imply that all dishonesty be overlooked? Would that not make matters worse?' objected Abeer.

'Matters are bad enough with what we're doing now. We are either ranting in anger at the corrupt, or, inured by their continual presence, being indifferent to them. That's no solution.'

'Then what is?' asked Raghu. He felt entitled to speak now. He was done with the necessary number of sentences that an outsider needs to hear before being inducted into a conversation.

'If you want a solution,' answered Mr Bajwa, 'you would need to strike at temptation itself. Impediments would need to be introduced between Adam and the apple; not only such impediments which make the apple more inaccessible, but also those which dissuade with the threat of inescapable consequences.'

'Whatever happened to self-control?' inquired Abeer.

'I think it was decidedly proven in the good garden that man has very little of it. And that, if you ask me, was the most important lesson from that episode.

'Think about it. Why does our country rank so high on the corruption index? What do the other developed nations have that we don't? I'll tell you. More vigilance, more accountability, and quick justice. This way, the seeds of corruption are relegated to an anaerobic environment. Only the few mutated ones are able to germinate.

'Coming back to the railway platform; your urge to pocket the pouch would've been considerably diminished if you were being watched by more electronic or human eyes.

'And hence, in leaving the money on the bookshelf, your mother was more at fault than the maid who took it. If we are to assume that the maid had till now been honest, what we have in fact done is taken away her scruples forever. We are thus guilty of initiating her into a life of theft.'

Mrs Bajwa took on a pensive hue. Her husband, wisely, decided not to press the point further. 'In a nutshell,' he said, turning to the boys, 'Ours is a perpetrator who's smug in the belief that no one will see him pick up the pouch of diamonds. What's more, he knows that even in case he's caught doing so—which can only be due to ill-luck or stupidity—conviction would be a far cry. And ultimately, he's well aware that should it actually come down to conviction, at least twenty years will need to elapse before the sentence is carried out. Who knows, prison at that age might turn out to be a better option than an old age home. More close friends around!'

'I think the boys have had enough for a day,' declared Mrs Bajwa. 'Also, I'm going to the kitchen to fetch them a second round of fruit cream. Let's see if any of your lectures can whip up a resistance to *that* temptation.'

Mr Bajwa laughed harder than usual. He knew he had a habit of getting carried away.

The passage

The academic year end arrived. Raghu and his classmates had been awaiting it eagerly. Owing to early board examinations, all seniors had left for vacations and the only students left on campus were those from grade seven and eight. Raghu's batch—grade eight—now hoped to rule the roost and henpeck the juniors. This was the way things had always been and, indeed, would have continued to be were it not for a little quirk of fate.

It turned out that there were more number of boys in the senior batch than the junior one. In other words, this was an army with more generals than foot-soldiers. So whenever a minion from grade seven was summoned to run an errand, it invariably emerged that he already had three at hand. Eventually, a junior without an errand became as rare as a phoenix.

Expectedly, the head-count ratio wasn't the only culprit behind the deluge of errands. Abetting it was a factor which advertisers fondly call 'a supply generated demand.' So fond had the nouveau-seniors become of their errand running facility that they were now *creating* errands.

No, these were not happy times for grade seven. And had it not been for an intervening providence—that supposedly whimsical force which in truth only seeks out healthy equilibriums—the sickbay would have been flooded with cases of fatigue collapse.

The intervention was nothing but a simple insight. The juniors soon realized that bogus errands were only to their advantage, and that an unfinished bogus errand could very effectively be used as an excuse for refuting an important one. The loophole came to be employed profusely and soon the whole system, in the manner of an overburdened judiciary, got clogged. Truce had to be proclaimed. Abhay declared that till a solution could be thought of, no junior was to be asked to run an errand of a personal nature. Only genuine housework or schoolwork was to be referred to them. The phoenix, though not risen, was at least breathing.

Though Shah and his ilk were not very pleased with the new arrangement, they stuck to it; because even in a democracy the voice of reason is occasionally adhered to. But only occasionally! Reason could not keep instinctive urges at bay for too long. Presently, the errand creators' patience started to wear out and their unused seniority began to itch. They felt like the owner of a newly acquired Ferrari which has been stranded on a busy and pitted road. And like that frustrated owner, they too restlessly sought an opportunity to fully unleash the newfound power. It was only a matter of time before they would invent an excuse for breaking some rule or the other. Indeed, such a time did not take long to arrive.

In Scad it was strictly prohibited for students to wander beyond campus limits. Shah and Co. decided that they would. It was planned that after evening roll call they would take the second school gate—the one that was meant for the general public and hence less guarded—to sneak away into town. They would have dinner at Quality, fruit cream at Volga, *paan* at Banarsi's, and top it all up with a movie at the Ritz. There was however just one hitch. The party guest-list did not boast of any celebrities.

In other words, there was no prefect-type material amongst those who had decided to abscond. The wily Shah realized that this was an anomaly that needed immediate rectification. In case they were caught, he reasoned, the prefects-in-the-pod would come handy in mitigating the ensuing punishment. There was no way the authorities could go heavy on a bunch of blue eyes.

Never one to waste time, Shah immediately set about recruiting the prefects. His technique was simple. C was roped in by being informed that A and B were on the list. B was enticed by using the names of A and C. And thus when it came to A, Shah didn't even have to lie.

An invitation was extended to Raghu as well. He duly accepted it, without once realizing that his doing so would upset Abeer.

'Give me one good reason why you're doing this,' demanded Abeer of Raghu.

'Uhh...you know...it seems like a nice movie. And of course...there's the grub.'

'In case you've forgotten, tomorrow's movie night. Why miss the one here and walk six kilometers for another?'

'Actually more than the movie it's the food thing. I'm tired of the mess stuff.'

'I have some tuck lying with me. Take it.'

Raghu wondered why solutions were readily available for fictitious predicaments; and why good friends bear this uncanny resemblance to one's conscience. 'Chaterji's going too,' he put in feebly, hoping that the mention of a prefect would somehow bolster his case.

'Abhay isn't,' shot back Abeer.

'But Chaterji...'

'Chaterji's been included for the same reason as you. But *he* is taking this trip out of his own sweet will.'

'So am I,' resisted Raghu.

'Really?' countered Abeer. He said that it in a tone that was neither accusing nor sarcastic, and Raghu was forced to answer the question in earnest. '*They* asked me so nicely, I couldn't refuse. Would've hurt their sentiments if I did.'

'All this long, *they* were shallow people with opinions that didn't matter. Now, they are people with sentiments—ones which cannot be hurt. Isn't that convenient? Branding people to be as good, or as bad, as their opinions about us are!' this was from Abhay who had arrived to hear the last part of their conversation.

Raghu opened his mouth to say something but then thought the better of it. He just turned away and left.

'You didn't have to be that harsh,' said Abeer to Abhay, 'I mean, why restart his them-phobia?'

''Coz it's better than a misguided them-philia,' countered Abhay.

'I'd still prefer the latter,' mumbled Abeer softly.

During the course of the next day neither Abeer nor Abhay pestered Raghu on the issue. Come evening and he was gone. When Abeer came casually strolling into the prep-room, Abhay—who had guessed the real reason for his being there—informed 'No need to look around. I saw him leave.'

Time went by very slowly for Abeer that evening and he could just about manage to stare through the movie. When he reached the hostel, he was surprised to see Shah already there.

'Back so early?' he enquired.

'Yup. The movie downtown was pathetic. We left it halfway. Takes care of the roll call as well.' The roll call was an occasional affair, for it was only seldom that the housemaster bothered to take attendance after the Saturday night movie. Yet, it was not something which could be ruled out. And it was to safely cover that contingency that Shah had made it back on time.

It was just as well that he had done so; because presently, the house-servant announced for everyone to be assembled in the hall. The roll call was on.

'Where's Raghu?' asked Abeer anxiously.

'He was trailing behind us. Should be here any time now,' replied Shah.

But the 'any time now' didn't happen soon enough. Attendance was taken and it came to be known that two people were missing— Raghu Kumar and Partho Chaterji. The housemaster, who went by the nickname of Pikku, was absolutely furious.

Pikku always expected circumstances to align themselves according to his wishes and needs. When circumstances didn't, like now, he interpreted it as a betrayal by destiny. His first reaction was always that of rage, invariably followed by self pity.

'Have them sent to my quarters the moment they arrive,' shouted Pikku. It never occurred to him that the absent boys could be in some kind of peril. In a Pikkucentric universe, all events were broadly classified into two basic categories. Events that were against him, and events that were not so much against him. Apart from that, an event had no other relevance.

The irate Pikku was walking away from the roll-call line when he heard the patter of running feet behind him. It was Raghu and Chaterji. 'Where were you?' he screamed at the top of his voice. Raghu was instantly frozen into silence. Chaterji wasn't. 'Had gone to the toilet, sir,' he answered with absolute sang froid. It was a foolproof alibi. What's more, Pikku knew that too. And thus deprived of the opportunity to even reprimand them, Pikku availed himself of the next best option—a sermon. He promptly launched into a rather elaborate one. Starting with 'punctuality' and then covering 'healthy eating habits', he was just about to make that perfect transition from constipation to diarrhea when suddenly, he spotted something.

'What's that in your pocket,' he asked Raghu, pointing menacingly at him.

'N...nothing sir,' was the instinctive answer.

'Out with it,' urged Pikku.

The 'it' was a wad of *paan*s—a small present for Abeer and Abhay. The soggy packet stained Raghu's hand as he drew it out, much in the same way that it had stained his pocket. Nothing could be done now. He was caught red handed.

'Who else was there with you?' demanded Pikku after he was done with the expected bout of gloating.

Obviously, Raghu was tempted to name everybody. Their sheer number would have obliterated the possibility of expulsion as a punishment. But somehow... 'Was Chaterji there with you?' roared Pikku once again. A few months back, in times when he hadn't yet met Abeer, it would have been really easy to answer that one. Raghu wondered why now it wasn't. This couldn't be the fear of being called a squealer—they called him all kinds of names anyway. Nor was it any sudden newfound love for Chaterji, Shah et al. Or was it? Much as he tried, Raghu couldn't figure out why exactly it didn't seem right to tell on his classmates. Especially Chaterji. It made a lot of sense to pull Chaterji down with him. Chaterji's father was an alumnus and the family's blue-eyed status was bound to rein in the punishment. And yet...

'So there was nobody with you?' bellowed Pikku. It was more of an accusation than a question. Because even though he really relished these episodes of castigation, his innate pusillanimity always sought that the number of adversaries be restricted to the bare minimum.

'No sir, there wasn't,' answered Raghu after a long pause.

For most guys who'd gone to town, that pause was nothing less than an eternity. For Raghu, it was the fading away of an epoch.

Raghu wasn't punished after all. Abhay, on the pretext of delivering some report to Pikku, casually apprised him with the repercussions of bringing the episode to the principal's notice. Their hostel's chances of claiming the annual best-hostel shield would be seriously marred. Pikku considered and was quick to reach a decision. In a Pikkucentric universe, it wasn't a difficult one.

Part II

New wings

Thanks to his caste quota, Raghu had cleared his IIT entrance and was poised to spend the next four years in Delhi. Incidentally, the four years would also yield him an engineering degree.

Abeer too had taken the IIT exam. His entrance-test marks were just a tad below cut-off but a couple of those ranked above him had opted out—probably to try-out for a better branch the following year. And this, along with the fact that there had been an inter-departmental seat-shuffle, facilitated Abeer's scraping through into the premier institute. He was well aware of the role providence had played in his success and was happy to acknowledge it, although somewhat coyly. 'When you really want something, the whole university conspires in helping you to achieve it.'

Abhay was already in Delhi. His father's ill-health and the family business had forced him to quit Scad after his eleventh grade. Unsurprisingly, he hadn't found the prospect of returning home an entirely disagreeable one. School had proved to be such a cakewalk that any sort of a real challenge was welcome.

'The name's Ghosh, Arindam Ghosh,' was how the long-haired, loud-shirted, battered-jeans-clad lad was introducing himself to some in the queue.

'Ah, the glib talking Mr Bond—the man with the golden gums,' whispered Raghu to Abeer as he pointed at Arindam in what he thought was a discreet manner.

It wasn't. Arindam caught sight of the pointing finger and paced forebodingly towards the duo. Raghu mentally braced himself for the inconvenience that was to follow, but thankfully, Arindam's first words turned out to be in an amicable vein, 'Extremely appropriate! Instead of the cold shoulder, you decide to give the man with the golden gums the...no, not the gold, but the coldfinger. And yes, the name is Ghosh. Arindam Ghosh. Friends call me Aari.' Both Abeer and Raghu had to smile. Aari smiled back. And a bond was instantly initiated.

The queue in question was the queue for room allotment. Aari, who for some reason had an idea of the 'wing' system in IIT, had been talent scouting for wing-mates. Wings, he explained to Raghu, were sections in the hostel building. Tacit tradition had it that people who stayed together in a wing during their first year were more or less doomed to stay with each other for the three subsequent years. Wings, went on Aari, hence determined the way one's character would shape up. Wings dictated the kind of job one would land up with at the end of four years. In fact, wings decided whether one's stay in IIT *would* be four years. And though Raghu thought that this was giving too much wing to imagination, he nevertheless found the idea of the four-year contract quite acceptable. Having Abeer around was of course a very agreeable prospect. And the Aari chap didn't look too bad either. Besides, he seemed to know his way around.

Raghu shot a glance towards Abeer. But even before Abeer

could articulate an approval, Aari announced, 'It's settled then. I'll take the both of you under my wing.'

Because the ask-hear-quip-laugh and humiliate schedule holds something of a universal appeal, ragging in IIT happened to be quite similar to that in Scad. If there was any difference, it lay in the presence of one additional feature—the fresher play. Each hostel was required to come up with an original and amusing one. Script, acting, direction—everything was supposed to be done by the freshers. So besides providing general amusement, the play also afforded the seniors an idea of the new crop.

Aari, as could be expected, got to take over the reins of the fresher play. But with ragging having scared off most freshers, rounding up prospective talent proved to be a difficult task even for him. He eventually had to simplify the selection process by taking in anybody whose vocal cords could muster up 45 decibels and above.

It was now for this loud lot to come up with a script.

'Let's enact some Santa Banta jokes,' suggested shorty spiked hair.

Aari looked at him severely. Since violence was not an alternative, he took the next best option. 'You the chap from Rohtak?' he asked. The intention was to make the guy feel like an absolute zero, and that was precisely the temperature of Aari's voice.

Spiked hair's silence went to show that he pleaded guilty to the accusation. He kept mum for the rest of the meeting. Though hailing from a small town was not really a matter of ignominy, it could sometimes be made to seem like one; at least during the small-towner's first year in the metro.

'What if we do a parody of some latest running hit,' suggested the guy from DPS. Being a Delhi-ite, he considered himself entitled to speak.

'Not a bad idea! Not bad at all. I'm otherwise pretty stingy with compliments but I must confess you're certainly not as dim as your face makes you out to be.' Having secured success with the rookie from Rohtak, Aari was now warming up to his true element.

'How very mean to say that,' commented blinking-brown-eyes, who Aari instantly recognized as the guy brought up under the watchful eye of two elder sisters. 'Mean' is not an adjective often employed by the un-fair sex.

A ripe little retort instantly sprang to Aari's mind, but along with it sprang a warning, a vaguely recollected caution imparted by some Lincoln guy—something about the unfeasibility of antagonizing all the people all the time. Aari decided that it would be prudent to consolidate.

'You misconstrue,' began the spin doctor. 'So allow me to explain that remark about your face. You see, we've been here about a month now. During this while we've interacted with at least a hundred new faces—faces that were handsome and faces that were the dog. Now it's against my discreet nature to take names but I'm sure you know the guys who at first impression had seemed very handsome. Then as they opened their mouths in profound stupidity, scales fell from our eyes.

'Conversely, there are these very ordinary looking guys who by dint of their personality have changed our perception of them. We now adore the very features that once seemed grotesque. The small eyes, the long nose, the scar on the cheek; all of these now add to character.

'The truth is friends that when it comes to men, the personality within renders the outer appearance transparent.'

As the assembled menagerie wasn't exactly comprised of hunks, it was rather pleased with this newfound knowledge. DPS boy was so mollified that he unleashed a plethora of suggestions for the play. Aari accepted them all.

Aari Ghosh was hugely fond of two things. Antagonizing people and indulging in arguments. He couldn't have chosen his hobbies more judiciously. They absolutely complemented each other. Antagonizing people led to arguments and arguments antagonized people. It was a perfect circle.

Aari never waited for people to take a stance (i.e., the pretext on which he could initiate an argument). He *ascribed* people with stances. For instance, just because he'd seen the Gita lying in Raghu's room, he conveniently assumed that Raghu was a staunch adherent. Never mind that the Gita was with Raghu solely on his mother's behest and that he had never read a page. The mere presence of the holy text was reason enough for Aari to direct even faintly religious arguments to Raghu. He did so even now.

'There goes your law of conservation of souls,' bellowed Aari as he barged into Raghu's room, newspaper in hand.

'Law of conservation of souls?' enquired Raghu, who was gradually learning not to be surprised at things that Aari said, or did.

'Yup. Your law in the Gita which says that the soul can neither be created nor destroyed, thus implying that the number of souls in the universe is constant. Then, I ask,' smiled Aari, carefully letting the cat out of the bag 'how do you explain this latest breakthrough in cloning? Where do you propose to get all those extra souls from?'

'I don't know,' replied Raghu at length. 'And I *also* don't know where they're getting the extra souls for a rapidly increasing population.' He was half irritated, half amused at Aari's penchant for converting all of life's intrigues into a problem of physics. And even though he wasn't at all eager to carry on the argument, he well knew there was no getting away from it. He reluctantly reconciled to play along. 'The soul Aari, if there is such a thing, isn't proclaimed to be a physical entity. And because it's *not* a physical entity, it would be safe to say that it doesn't exist in numbers or volumes. Therefore, your law of conservation would scarcely apply to it.'

Aari was not one to cede an argument so easily. Swift came the interjection. 'But if the soul doesn't exist in numbers, why's it always said that man has *a* soul. That is, one soul. Or do you contest that? Do your rabbi's and priests and padres stock up more than one soul by virtue of their being more enlightened than the rest of you?'

'If anybody needs an extra helping of soul Aari, it's you. I'm sure the one originally issued is in tatters by now.'

Aari smiled. It was the smile that is often the precursor to the last laugh. 'How could it be in tatters when your *Gita* says that weapons cannot harm it, water cannot inundate it, fire cannot burn it...'

Raghu couldn't help laughing, if only at the jejuneness of the conversation. 'Well I know of one good thing that fire does burn,' he said. And they promptly shared a cigarette.

Rendezvous

Rendezvous, the IIT annual festival, had arrived. This was much needed relief for freshers after a long month of ragging. However, not all freshers had the good fortune of fully availing of this godsend. In accordance with an age-old tradition, a number of them were drawn away into taking 'volunteer' jobs. These were guys whose lot it was to help out with the execution of Rendezvous. And though their rationale for agreeing to do so was something on the lines of '*someone's* got to work behind the show', the real reason obviously lay in their desire to fit in. It lay in their inability to turn down influential seniors who'd asked to be assisted. Luckily, before any such difficult choices could descend upon Raghu or Abeer, they came upon some priced info.

'Remember, security is the thing to volunteer for. That's where the power is,' was Aari's sage advice to the two of them.

'Well good for you. There will now be one less contender for power,' declared Abeer. Then in response to the eyebrow raised by Raghu, he went on to add, 'I think I'll use the holidays to visit home.'

'Are you crazy? The place will be swarming with females. Rendevous implies doing the P.Y.T., and not the T.Y.P.,' said an astounded Aari.

'P.Y.T. I think would be Pretty Young Things. What's T.Y.P.?

asked Abeer.

'Travelling to Your Parents.'

'Well don't worry,' laughed Abeer. 'You will have Raghu for company.' The seemingly casual remark was intended to save Raghu from the dilemma of accompanying him.

With just the slightest curl of his lips, Raghu provided the acknowledgement.

'Passes please,' barked Raghu at the bunch of girls waiting to be let in. The event had started and the other security volunteers were inside the auditorium. He alone had been asked to stay outside to handle latecomers.

One of the girls thrust out a wad of passes and simultaneously signaled the gang to proceed inside. 'Just a minute,' intervened Raghu. 'Allow me to count.'

'These geeks, I swear!' murmured one and Raghu instantly became extra cautious with his counting. The meticulousness paid off.

'There's one pass less. I'm afraid one of you will have to stay back.'

'Oh c'mon, we're sorry about that remark. She did not mean it,' pleaded the leader of the pack.

'The remark has nothing to do with it,' lied Raghu.

A lot of cajoling, reasoning and beseeching followed. But Raghu did not budge. It was with little hope that one of the girls made a final attempt.

'How can you expect one person to go back all by herself? And we said we're sorry.'

'Then perhaps you could do with a bit of repentance.'

Very seldom does it happen that a man dons an imposing robe of power and doesn't eventually begin to mistake it for his own skin. First-time power bearers are even less discriminating. They make that mistake with mere rags as well.

But to his credit, Raghu repented those words within a moment of uttering them. What added to his torment was the fact that he couldn't even comprehend the rationale behind his unreasonable behavior. This type of conduct was not characteristic of him at all. And yet, strangely, even as his conscience pricked him for his unseemly behaviour, a part of him was relishing it. It was in a way like compulsive eating. Like a morsel being munched, the utterance gave pleasure while on the tongue; and regret, once it had left it.

The girls had been pushed to arrive at a decision and they were now out with one.

'All right,' said the girl who'd been doing most of the talking, 'if that's the way you insist.'

Passes were handed over once again and all but one girl proceeded to enter.

Having spent years in boarding school camaraderie, this was not an outcome that Raghu had anticipated. At first he thought that this was merely a ploy to melt him into submission. He could even visualize the course of events: the lone girl being allowed entrance, she joining her gang, and then the giggles. Big-time giggles. And giggles scared Raghu.

By the time he returned to the real world, the girl who was left behind had walked away. He looked at her lone figure fading away gradually into the night and was instantly filled with remorse. He at once wanted to undo the way he'd acted.

'Listen,' he shouted. But the girl kept walking.

'Excuse me.' Still no response.

He knew that if he went up to the girl it would be at the cost of abandoning his post. He had been strictly instructed not to do so. Yet, the moment he saw her disappear around the corner, his heart was imbued with that Pascal-esque quality—it started to harbour reasons of its own which the head knew nothing about. All concern for the consequences began to fade. He took off in the direction of his victim. When he caught up with her he was breathing far more heavily than what the distance warranted.

'I say, please stop,' urged Raghu, even as he made a mental note to cut down on the smoking.

'What is it?' she asked irritably.

'Please listen to me.'

The girl stopped and turned around. The streetlight now fell directly on her face and Raghu could clearly see the tears that glistened in those large eyes.

'I was s-s-saying,' he stammered 'You may go in with your friends if you like.'

But even before the girl could articulate a refusal, Raghu knew. He knew it was no longer about attending the event in the auditorium. His pre-Abeer memories from Scad came back in a flash. Memories about the pain of being the redundant member in a group; memories about the ignominy of moving around with a gang and being the butt of all its ridicule; but worst of all, memories of having to continually maneuver the fig leaf of hope lest those tacit arrangements become explicit. And by his one act of meaningless authority Raghu had just ripped off that fig leaf.

'See, I'm sorry,' he said abruptly, and as if the apology made him a smaller person, was quick to add, 'More sorry for what has happened than for what I did.' Then better sense gradually trickled in and he saw himself for the egoistical pig he was being, and he once again scurried to amend his statement. What ensued was an incoherent mumble. Finally, all he could do was close his eyes in disgust. When he opened them, it was to just gaze. He gazed at the girl and hoped that his eyes would do the talking.

Now since writers are often guilty of attributing too much to 'earnest eyes', readers on their part have learnt to counter that ruse using the Santa Claus treatment—knowing it's not there, but pretending to believe.

Earnest eyes, however, must have had a definite role to play in the present case. Because otherwise, there was no reason why the girl should have smiled. A faint smile it was, only slightly more explicit than the one which had made, and makes, Mr Da Vinci famous.

'It's okay,' she said

'It *will* be okay,' she added after a pause. But even though her tone was self assuring, her timid eyes belied the brave façade of her words.

There is something about 'Damsels in deemed distress' and 'Guys of wayward ways with a supposed heart of gold'. They have always been able to elicit love out of even their most inured and hardened counterparts. And Raghu was hardly a man with a proven track record of being hard of heart. He didn't stand a chance. Transfixed, he looked on at her figure bathed in rich yellow light; he looked at her timid eyes, her rippling hair, her fluttering skirt, her fingers held near the brow to arrest an errant tear that might want to escape. No, Raghu definitely did not stand a chance. And cupid played farmer in a heart that had for too long been lying fallow.

'My name's Raghu,' he informed.

'I'm Lila,' she replied.

'Beautiful name.'

'I somehow knew you were going to say so.' She burst into a little laugh as she said that, and the suddenness of that movement caused a welled up tear to run off.

God! It was the most beautiful laughter he'd ever heard. He wanted to tell her that but stopped himself in the nick of time. With one cliché already on his account, he couldn't risk another. It was just last week that *Scent of a Woman* had made a splash at the movie festival. Plagiarizing a line by Al Pacino was fraught with too much risk; especially because he too was going blind in love. He wanted to put *his* best foot forward, not somebody else's. Raghu toyed with some witty remarks but then decided against using any of them. He resolved to be at least as honest as the situation permitted.

'You see, all my previous education has been in an all-boys' school. I really do not know how to converse with girls. Till date I've been with just three girls my age.'

'You shouldn't be boasting, Raghu,' she smiled.

What was it about one's name, wondered Raghu. Why did its phonetics change so drastically when uttered from the honeyed tongue of the adored one.

'You misunderstand,' he smiled back, 'By "been", I mean like held a two-sentence conversation with these girls. In fact, should you choose to reply to what I'm saying right now, sheer verbosity will make you the girl I've been most intimate with.'

Lila laughed. An even better laugh this time, thought Raghu.

As the ensuing silence prolonged, Raghu became nervous. Was she deliberately keeping mum because of what he had said?

'Can I drop you to your hostel?' he asked abruptly. Nothing else had come to mind.

'I guess that's the least you can do for a girl you're most intimate with.' Their eyes met for the briefest span as she said that. A span not long enough to warrant a commitment. And yet not short enough to prevent kindling the hopes of one.

Raghu hailed an auto rickshaw upon reaching the institute gate. As he reluctantly stepped into that unromantic vehicle, he made a spot decision. Far away in a different time zone, little did his parents realize that their savings would soon be set back by the cost of a motorbike.

The trip to Lila's hostel was rather prosaic. Auto-rickshaws do that. All that the two of them could exchange was some very routine and cursory information. Somehow, they could also manage to exchange their phone numbers.

In foreign territory

The Copernican model of a geocentric universe must have been an easy one to conceive. The model, after all, is a natural extrapolation of the self-centric instinct and the unrealistic levels of self importance which most men harbour.

So when Raghu—after being kicked out of security on charges of absconding—walked his long Roberto Baggio walk from the institute area to his hostel, it appeared to him that all people he met on the way were reacting to his circumstances. Some were mocking him, some were pitying him, and yet others—they being decent people—were deliberately keeping their eyes averted to save him the embarrassment. Raghu was absolutely sure that all these people actually knew him. Hell, who in his right mind could fail to recognize a high and mighty security volunteer! And who could fail to notice that that volunteer had been stripped of his very ostentatious 6 cm by 1.5 cm batch? Yes, everything was in the open now. His fall from grace was there for all to see.

Under the circumstances, the only escape Raghu could think of was to confine himself to his hostel room. He did just that for the weekend. Of course, the option of a city outing was always at hand but the snag in that was want of company. Abeer was out of town and the rest of his batchmates were basking in the novelty of Rendezvous. Raghu considered giving Lila a call but with his self confidence at an all-time low, that idea was doomed from inception.

'All dressed down and nowhere to go!' was how Raghu summed up the situation of his wasted weekend. It could be said that he got what he deserved, for such over the top self-consciousness is hardly justifiable in a person of above average intelligence. But before that indictment, it should be ascertained whether a correlation between self-consciousness and intellect actually exists. Indeed, close examination reveals that there's no discernible correspondence between the two. Self-consciousness—like most afflictions—picks its victims indiscriminately from all across the intellect-spectrum. So at one end is the case of the recluse genius who over-analyzes all speech (the genius who by peeling the onion of his uttered words keeps scrutinizing all underlying layers of possible implication, without for one moment realizing that the person to whom such words were said has neither the inclination nor the leisure or capacity for such complex endeavour.) And on the other end is the more mundane matter of the average Jane—and in an increasingly metrosexual world, Joe too—who strongly believes that the sole function of public memory is to keep track of the outfits she sports. Not for her, then, to be seen dead in attire which she has worn at any of the previous twelve outings. Of course, when asked whether *she* remembers what an acquaintance wore in their last-but-one meeting, the answer drawn is invariably a blank.

Raghu's behaviour may have been drastic, but it was definitely explicable.

Abeer arrived Sunday evening. He spent an hour talking to Raghu about things in general before he popped the question. 'What's her name?'

'What's whose name?' fumbled a surprised Raghu.

Abeer did not reply. There was no need. Given how well they knew each other, a short silence is all it took to reiterate the futility of pretensions.

'Aari?' asked Raghu. He always had a hunch that Aari had seen them on the street that night.

'Aari,' nodded Abeer.

'Her name's Lila,' said Raghu softly. 'But there's nothing to it of what you're thinking,' he was quick to add.

Guys seldom confess of love that is nascent. It is basic insecurity masquerading as machismo.

'She hasn't even called after that night,' continued Raghu, now trying to make amends for his earlier reticence.

'Well in that case *you* could have called her. You took her number, didn't you?' inquired Abeer.

'I bet she didn't give it to him,' boomed Aari, who'd just materialized out of nowhere. He had this weird habit of eavesdropping outside rooms which he eventually intended to enter. Also, he didn't believe in knocking; he would just wait for the opportune moment and make his entry.

'Did she?' pressed Aari, not willing to let go of the dynamic impact of his entry.

'Yes she did. 662504,' said Raghu in reflex, and almost immediately regretted having played into Aari's hands.

'That, my friend, could hardly be termed as classified information. As half of Delhi University will tell you, that's the LSR hostel number. Won the MTNL award last year for being in perpetual use. But anyway, we'll give you credit because *she* gave you that number.'

'You seem to know *everything*!' smiled Abeer as he got up to leave. 'Raghu will be a much enlightened person by the time I'm done with my shower.'

Aari took the praise at face value. 'Forget an unengaged phone line during primetime, 7 to 11 p.m.,' he began. 'Mealtimes are good, that is if she's willing to sacrifice her fare for you: which by the way is excellent in their mess. Your best bet would be just after classes. However, all said and done, I still think that a pair of wheels would be swifter than telecommunication. But since you don't own such a pair, and remittances from the UK will take about a fortnight to arrive, yours truly will be kind enough to lend you *kaali ghodi*.' *Kaali ghodi* was what Aari called his motorbike.

Aari was a man who harboured a genuine interest in other people's affairs. The fact that Raghu did not appear inclined to talk did in no way induce him to abandon post. He simply picked up another vein.

'Talking of the UK, have always wanted to ask you this. Tell me, what kept you from studying there? I mean most of us are slogging our asses off for scholarships in western universities. And you walked away from what was provided to you on a platter. Why?'

'I prefer here,' replied Raghu tersely. Despite his reluctance, there were two reasons why he went along with that conversation. One, the generous motorbike offer from Aari. And two, not talking about this would have meant talking about Lila.

'Ah, he prefers here! And may we ask why? UK not good enough for you?' warmed up Aari.

'U.K.'s excellent. But...'

'But?'

'But it's somehow not home.'

'Now that's interesting. Never knew of that patriotic streak in you.'

'It has nothing to do with patriotism.'

'Racism then?'

'Uhhh…not exactly. Not to say there's no racism in UK but luckily my family hasn't met with anything dire.'

'Then what *is* it?' asked an impatient Aari.

Raghu regretted not picking one of Aari's reasons. He was now required to come out with the real one, or allow Aari to pester it out of him.

'It's actually something rather silly,' offered Raghu hesitantly.

'I'm sure it isn't,' said Aari, trying to look very serious. He was sensing some masala here and didn't want to chuck it with a premature laugh.

'When I was studying in London…' started out Raghu, and then paused instinctively. Then realizing that he was already committed to the conversation, he decided to go on. This time he began with a disclaimer, 'You know those stupid prejudices which form for no reason at all? And then they turn into a mental block and you're never able to see beyond them?'

So earnest was Aari's nod of understanding that Raghu came to the story straight away. 'It was a winter morning and I was fooling around with a couple of kids at school. Brits, all of them. They were mock smoking—blowing out their breaths and seeing the vapours condense. Now you wouldn't believe this but when I tried to do the same it simply wouldn't happen. The vapour just wouldn't condense! The kids found it very funny that I couldn't smoke and promptly made me the butt of their jokes. The harder I blew to redeem myself, the louder they laughed. It was then that I knew I was different. I knew that I would never blend in with the mainstream, and that the mainstream would never blend in with me. The very air of England had declared it so.'

'Do you even realize how crazy you sound, Kumar? And how childish is your prejudice?'

'Who told you prejudices don't grow with us? As a matter of fact, we even provide them a sanctuary for doing so without restraints. How we rush to plaster with new reasoning any crack of fallibility that has begun to show!'

'But for *your* particular prejudice, no amount of plastering could possibly be enough. Times have changed and the world has been reduced to a global village. Those differences you talk of have been torn down by all those global citizens out there.'

'Aari, let me apprise you of a fact. There's no such thing as a global citizen.'

'I could give you umpteen examples.'

'All your examples would be about people who are super rich, famous, or influential. Or, there isn't much cultural difference between their stations of origin and destination.'

'Last point taken. But what could richness or fame have to do with being a global citizen?'

'There was this person called Leo Tolstoy. You might have heard of him. He used to say that all happy people are happy alike, but all unhappy people are unhappy in their different ways. Common people like us, who face reality in its multifaceted avatars, can never seamlessly mesh the realities of two diverse cultures. There are too many loose ends to be taken care of and each of them has to be addressed stitch by painful stitch. Conversely, because the super rich of the world have to address far fewer facets of reality, the differences between them are fewer. For them, the meshing of two different fabrics is pretty smooth. It's only occasionally that the intervening gaps show.'

The two were quiet for some time before Raghu remarked, 'It's a fact you can't run away from. The globe *does* comprise of different ethnic groups.'

Aari came up close to Raghu and acted as if he were searching for something on his face.

'What the hell are you doing?' asked Raghu.

'Looking for a hint of that toothbrush moustache fuehrer,' was the answer.

'Borrowing your own phrase...you misconstrue. I never said anything about the superiority of one ethnic group over another. All I said was they are different.'

'And what kind of differences would you be talking of?'

'Well eating habits, dressing habits, sleeping habits...'

'Habits all!' said Aari triumphantly. 'Habits aren't something which cannot be changed.'

'Agreed. But there are other things too. Things more subtle than habit.'

'For example?'

'For example...' fumbled Raghu.

'Not able to put your thoughts into words?' mocked Aari.

'Not able to put my perceptions into thoughts.'

'C'mon, one example,' goaded Aari.

'Sense of humour, for one,' hazarded Raghu after some thought.

'Sense of humour?'

'Yes. Sense of humour. All ethnic groups have a distinct sense of humour, though sometimes the subtlety in shade may not be so discernible. But I'm sure that if we had an expert on humour, like that Pygmallion guy was on accents, he could tell.'

'So you don't want to settle in the UK because they won't laugh at your jokes?'

'I knew something that puerile was coming up.'

'Okay, I'm sorry. But why would sense of humour be so important?'

'That's not the point. The point is that this difference in sense of humour is not a coincidence. It's there for a reason. It's a subtle manifestation of more deeply rooted societal mores. What we laugh at gives us away. It tells of our values, our levels of sophistication, our societal structures, our taboos...'

'I think you're overdoing it,' objected Aari before Raghu could finish. 'I see no connection between sense of humour and values.'

'But it's obvious. Just think about it. We laugh at things which—though seemingly absurd—are acceptable to us at some level. We don't laugh at jokes that tell of anathematic transgressions.'

'And what's it about sense of humour and societal structures?' persisted Aari.

'Just watch any of the popular stage plays from across the border. Most of their humour is derived out of insulting the other guy. It's about laughing *at*, and not laughing *with*. And isn't that quite the case with Pakistani polity?'

It was some time before Raghu spoke again. 'You see, all I'm saying is that one's ethnicity and culture will always find ways to sprout to the surface. Sense of humour is just one such outlet. There would be many more, especially those which involve emotion in its raw form. And though you may manage to plug the obvious outlets of stark habits, the subtle ones are impossible to deal with—for the simple reason that they usually function involuntarily.'

'But just suppose,' began Aari with the ghost of a sneer, and Raghu knew from experience that he'd come up with, what *he* considered, an argument clincher, 'that a fair-complexioned Indian infant were to be adopted by British parents. Assuming that the boy's neighbors and skin did not inform him of the adoption, how would this boy fare? Would he, as you call it, *blend* in?'

'I wouldn't know. But yes, there is a high chance he would.'

'Then so would a fourth generation immigrant whose family has made efforts in that direction.'

'Perhaps.'

'So you do agree that ethnicity and culture are essentially about upbringing.'

'Upbringing, of course, is of crucial importance. It is upbringing that forms the primary bond which we have with our ethnicity and culture. And yet I'm inclined to believe that there also exists a secondary bond—something more subtle and intangible, a bond that has to do with heredity and genetics.'

'Bullshit!'

'Well many philosophers think that even language is genetically embedded. But we'll let that be. Let me rather tell you something from my direct experience.

'It's about the first time I traveled alone out of the UK. The flight was routed through Belgium and had an eight-hour stopover there. Eight long hours of utter boredom and homesickness. More importantly, eight long hours of insecurity about my boarding-school life ahead. I guess that is what triggered the small bout of xenophobia. I looked around and to my surprise there were no Indian looking faces in the whole airport. It was nothing like Southall where you could do half your shopping in Hindi. I was getting really uncomfortable and was on the verge of asking the ground staff whether I could call up my parents. Then, I saw it. In a corner of this lounge for unaccompanied minors there lay a magazine. Its front-page was half covered and all that was visible was the top half of a woman's face. Her eyes, her forehead, and in the middle of that forehead, a *bindi*. A red prominent *bindi*. I cannot describe the kind of assurance that *bindi* brought. Whether it was the assurance of motherhood—my mother uses a *bindi* sometimes—or that of a familiar image in a foreign land, I cannot say. But yes, it *was* an overwhelming emotion. How, I ask you, could a photograph of a *bindi* do that? As yet my association with a *bindi*, my primary bond with it, had been minimal. I had simply viewed it as an accessory used by some Indian women. Then how could this insignificant symbol of my ethnicity and culture evoke such strong emotions? Was it the genetic signature of my forefathers that had chosen this moment to unfold? Or was it something similar to what Jung refers to as the "collective unconscious"? What it was, I wouldn't know. So I simply choose to call it the secondary bond.'

'Man, you were one impressionable kid,' laughed Aari. Raghu laughed too.

'But tell me honestly,' began Aari in a different tone, as if to pull back Raghu into the real, more practical world. 'All this blending-shlending funda apart, wouldn't you like to settle in the UK just for the beautiful English countryside? So picturesque, so pristine! Say, is it actually the way they show it in the magazines and movies?'

Raghu laughed. 'Oh yes. It's very much the way they show it in the magazines and the movies. Better, if anything. When the sun comes up to dry the scenery that the rain has just washed, it's simply glorious to drive your way through it.'

'One could drive through such scenery for hours.'

'Uhhh….not hours. One hour would be more like it. Because that is about the time when I start noticing that something's seriously missing from the beautiful picture.'

'What?' asked a surprised Aari.

'A small roadside dhaba. The kind that specializes in densely concocted *chai* in glass tumblers. Not to mention piping hot *anda parathas* served with an unhygienic *achar*. In fact, I think I'll go and treat myself to some of those right now. Care to join? My treat.'

'Yup, by all means. Now this is what I most like about you Kumar. For all the crazy crap that you dole out, you manage to wash it off well with such welcome endings. Insti gate ho!'

As the two walked towards the institute gate to the *paratha* stall, Aari came up with his final query for the day, 'If you are so against the idea of settling abroad, does it not bother you that your parents are there?'

Raghu waited a while before answering. 'Not so much. They're there for professional reasons. The 'twain meets to make ends meet.'

Ho gaya

As always, Aari had been right. It was only in the afternoon that Raghu was able to get across to Lila on the public phone. To do so, he had had to bunk his foundry-shop practicals. 'But that's no bunk at all,' Abeer had teased, 'you'll be forging a relationship instead.'

So accustomed had Raghu become to the phone's busy tone that he was actually surprised when his call went through. His impulse was to hold on to the receiver tightly, as if to stop the tone from slipping away into busy mode again. Presently, a voice answered. Raghu informed whom he wanted to talk to and soon the name Lila Bharadwaj rang out on the public address system. Raghu had the receiver glued to his ear to such an extent that he could clearly hear the flutter of steps that preceded Lila's arrival on the phone. 'Hello?' she said.

'This is good,' thought Raghu. 'Her "Hello" is a question and that implies she's not frequent with the phone. In all probability, she isn't seeing anybody.'

'Hello,' he answered back. 'Raghu here.'

'Huh?'

'God! Had she forgotten?' he thought.

'Raghu. Uh…we…uh…met…' he couldn't bring himself to say anything further. It would have been tantamount to pleading.

'Raghu! I'm sorry the line is not very clear.'

'Whew! She remembers,' he said to himself.

'Then we shouldn't be putting your unclear line to further strain. Let's meet up. I have two tickets for this movie in PVR.'

'Now you didn't need to rush it that fast. And which tickets do you have, you moron? Will now have to talk to Aari to take care of that,' he thought.

'Tickets in hand, huh. So either you're taking me for granted or all your three girls have turned you down.'

'She remembers the three girls!' he thought.

'I would never dream of taking you for granted. And hence it must be my three girls who've turned me down.'

'What reason did they give?' she asked.

'No reasons. A plain no. Didn't I tell you, I share a very laconic relationship with them,' he answered.

Lila laughed.

'Man! Do they have a school where they teach girls to laugh that way? And if they do, should they really be letting them loose without a statutory warning display?' he said to himself.

'Those girls with me the other day,' Lila continued, 'they were saying you were nowhere to be seen during the festival.'

'That's because I was kicked out of security. For going A.W.O.L.'

'You didn't have to accentuate that, you idiot,' he cursed himself.

'I'm sorry. All because of me, I guess,' said Lila very softly.

'Now, look what you've done,' he thought.

'Oh c'mon. It wasn't the kind of job I'd give my right arm for.'

Lila didn't reply and the silence lingered. Then, in a very soft voice, Raghu spoke, 'But coming to think of it, I would.'

Inaudible to Raghu, Lila let out what could be termed as

an 'exhile'. An 'exhile' is a smile of humble beginnings which, with the aid of a sudden and short exhalation of air, is swiftly transformed into a small laugh. Earnest avatars of smiles can be employed for a variety of purposes—including display of empathy, response to humour, ironic detachment, and indications of happiness. An exhile is reserved mainly for happiness.

'By the way, are your tickets for a matinee show?' asked Lila.

'Of course.'

'I thought as much.'

Once the time to pick her up was fixed, Raghu placed the receiver on the cradle. Wasn't all this happening too fast, he wondered? Rendezvous; the security thing; him being posted out on that fateful night; the institute's yellow streetlights; a bit of Aari rubbing off, as a result of which, him being so brash and outspoken with her. Yes, this was definitely a case of the university conspiring.

The trip to the movies was rife with all the elements that Raghu could have hoped for. To begin with, Aari's bike—which Raghu had borrowed for the afternoon—was one that had been deprived of its rear handle-bar at a very early age. (Aari prided himself in such adjustments.) This meant that Lila had only Raghu to clutch onto for support while riding. She duly did so and for once in his life Raghu wasn't at all unhappy with the rundown roads. Potholes seemed like spring blossoms to him and he picked them aplenty as he rode along. It was only as they neared their destination that consequences began to dawn. He figured she would be holding him responsible for the missing handle-bar. Cheap, was how she would label him. Licentious was acceptable. Cheap wasn't.

No sooner had he parked the bike and taken off his helmet than he blurted out, 'This isn't my bike. Borrowed it from a friend.'

Lila burst out laughing at his naiveté. 'And to think that I was heaping the credit on you!' she said coyly.

On their walk towards the movie-hall, Raghu was abruptly greeted by the cigarette-stall owner on the sidewalk. '*Ho gaya?*' the stall owner inquired, and Raghu mumbled '*Ho gaya*' as he increased his pace, not a little embarrassed. This stall was one of the many spots which Aari and Raghu had scouted the previous evening while foraging for tickets. The movie in question was a blockbuster and tickets at the counter had long sold out. Secondary means, like the aforementioned cigarette-stall, had to be resorted to. However, merely having an access to such means wasn't an end to the problem. The challenge was after all a two-fold one. It involved making tickets available *and* keeping the premium cost affordable. This latter complexity had been handled by Aari with characteristic adroitness. He had freely narrated Raghu's budding love story to all and sundry. When Raghu had protested and asked whether there was any real need to do so, Aari had answered that there indeed was. There was a need because, according to Aari, 'the world loves a lover.'

The stall owner whom they had just met was an occupant of such a world. He was eager for a successful consummation of the love story and had therefore been vocal with his concern.

'A friend of your bike friend?' asked Lila gesturing towards the stall owner.

Raghu looked at her in stark disbelief.

'There's no need to be surprised, Raghu. This is my third year in Delhi. I know that this movie's a hit, making tickets hard to come by. And I know the usual spots where they're got.'

'Third year in Delhi? I thought you're from Lucknow.'

'Yes I am. Third year in Delhi because it's my third year in college,' she explained. Then after a short silence, added, 'Is that a problem with you?'

The question went unheard as Raghu tried to absorb this newfound information of her being elder than him. Then in a flash, Raghu's eyes lit up. Lit up like never before. 'Is…that…a …problem…with…you,' he meticulously repeated the words, savoring each syllable as he did so. 'Tell me,' he continued 'Do all girls propose like this?'

'Don't flatter yourself, fresher,' mumbled an embarrassed Lila.

The movie turned out to be worth its hype. But for Raghu, the real delight lay in watching the screen lights play out their myriad games on Lila's face. There of course was also the customary brushing of hands as they dipped into the popcorn bag—of which Raghu had bought only one on Aari's sage advice. However, the instances that stood out head and shoulders above the rest were when she missed out on a dialogue. At each of her inquiring glance, he drew up close and whispered in her ear. No, never again in his life would he so relish the feel of human hair on his face.

All in all, the Hollywood flick experience turned out to be of that same ethereal stuff which those movies are made of. Universal Studios too had joined the conspiracy.

'Maths shouldn't be difficult for a person of your intelligence,' said Raghu. He and Lila were taking a stroll in Deer Park.

'It's not a question of difficulty. I've just hated Maths right from my childhood,' she replied.

'But why?'

'I find it too definite. Everything's exact.'

'And what's wrong with exact?'

'Exactness puts a seal of finality on everything. Doesn't leave any loose ends for hope.'

'You're crazy,' Raghu laughed.

'That's what my father says, especially when I give him this same reason for not wanting to meet that astrologer of his.'

'Wow. Astrologers don't star in my list of favorite people either.'

'What's *your* reason?' asked Lila.

'It's simple. They tell me something good, I'm happy momentarily. They tell me something bad, it's always there at the back of my mind. And worst of all, if their one prediction for the good comes true, the lure for more ensures my perpetual enslavement to them.'

'Moreover,' interjected Lila, 'the best case scenario's no better. I'm talking of the scenario where they give you a prediction that is all good and you know it will all come true. Now wouldn't that make life so listless? I mean, life is wonderful because of its uncertainties. It's wonderful because anything great *can* happen to us in the time to come. If an astrologer were to tell me that something great *will* happen to me at such and such date, that's taking the fun away.'

'Is it?'

'Of course. Because then life till that date is reduced to a lesser life. Besides, no matter what fate one meets at that appointed date, disappointment is almost certain. Destinations are never worth the hype that their long wait creates.'

'Funny,' said Raghu after some consideration.

'What is?' she asked.

'How two people can reach the same conclusion by diametrically opposite reasoning. We have the same view of astrology; I, because of my pessimism, and you, because of the eternal optimist that you are.'

'True,' she smiled.

'You know, I really envy your optimism,' said Raghu after a pause.

'Don't worry. If we stay together long enough, it'll rub onto you.'

'Mmmmmm…can't wait for the rubbing,' said Raghu with as much lewdness in his voice as Lila's expression would permit.

'We were talking about Maths,' hurried Lila, immediately regretting her choice of words.

'The imminence of multiplication, among other things,' put in Raghu. Sensing Lila on the backfoot, he was in no mood to give up.

She needed to seek another angle to get him off track. She tried praise. 'Numbers are so beyond me Raghu. God, if I could just rent a bit of your mathematical mind.'

'Rent my mind? But you already *are* a tenant. 24/7,' persisted Raghu with a grin.

Lila tilted her head and smiled. Raghu, getting carried away with it, started to put his arm around her waist as he asked, 'But I still don't understand why you're so hell-bent on an MBA.' It was an essay type question which was meant to distract her from his maneuver. It didn't.

'For one thing,' said Lila as she un-wrapped his arm, 'an MBA would brace me to ward off hostile takeovers.'

The tick-off offended Raghu. He immediately withdrew into a broody silence. Lila didn't say anything either and the ambiance began to charge up with the pent-up energy of a first tiff. But since there's only so much charge that an ambiance of first love can sustain, it didn't take long for sparks to fly. Soon, Lila snuggled up to Raghu and planted a kiss on his lips. Yes, planted. Because that is exactly the way a first kiss behaves—growing so fast at first, then lingering in the mind in the years that follow.

Bottled up spirits

'Let's get drunk,' said the stranger standing at Raghu's door with a bottle of scotch in hand.

'Abhay!' shouted Raghu in delight as he shot up from his chair and rushed to hug him.

Abeer followed. His joy upon seeing Abhay was equally great, if not as apparent.

It being that half hour before dinner which hostelites generally idle away, a couple of guys from the wing were sitting chatting in Raghu's room. All of them were considerate enough to allow privacy to old friends and left within minutes of Abhay's arrival. Aari left too, but with a rider.

'I'll go arrange for the soda and accessories,' were the simple words with which he bustled into the *daru* party that was to follow.

Abhay's expression as he saw Aari walk out was not exactly one of distaste. Nevertheless, Abeer understood. 'Oh don't worry about him, he's okay. A bit loud mouthed, but okay,' he explained.

'But where have you been?' butted in Raghu, 'We've called up your number so many times. Just get to talk to your father. You always seem to be out of town.'

'Yes, work has been engaging,' answered Abhay.

'And the results?' asked Raghu.

'They're trickling in.'

'Just trickling?'

'Few more things need to be put in order.'

'Few things as in?'

'Few things as in the labour union, the middle management, the financiers.'

'That doesn't leave out much, does it?' laughed Abeer.

'Uhh...perhaps it does. Business is about more than all that,' said Abhay. Then after a pause, and with a change in expression, added 'So, how have the two of you been faring? Tell me all.'

Raghu did so with gusto and the mundane conversation served well to brush away a lot of dust that had settled upon the unattended friendship.

Aari's arrival was met with a silence. Though it was nothing more than a conversational break which the three had stumbled upon, it carried sufficient potential for damage. A sensitive person was likely to interpret that silence as conspiratorial. Aari, fortunately, was not a sensitive person. As he laid the contents of his shopping on the table, he warmed up to Abhay with characteristic ease 'These guys talk a lot about you and your Scad days,' he began.

'Raghu was telling me a lot about *you*,' answered Abhay.

'You shouldn't trust him. He's too generous with his praise,' came back Aari. What followed was a polite little laugh from Raghu—just as made-up as Aari's retort. New presences and correspondingly tweaked circumstances can have the strangest effects on people.

'But really, all this mutual praise is just smoke and mirrors. What I need to know is whether Mr. Kumar has been equally generous with his praise for the lady.' Aari had very adroitly steered the conversational ball into an area that could involve him. Had he not done so, there was every danger that the three would have regressed into their Scad days.

Abhay shot an inquiring glance at Raghu, seeing which, Aari concluded 'I thought as much.'

Good humored banter followed, all of it at Raghu's expense. In a group of friends, realized Raghu, it is advisable not to be the first to fall in love. Such a Romeo's fate is pretty similar to that of the person who first takes a bath in the haunted house of a horror movie.

Raghu figured that there was just one way to get Aari off his back. He had to entice him to speak about himself. He blatantly played that card.

'We've heard enough about lesser mortals. So why don't you tell us something about your own affairs...I mean, literally,' posed Raghu to Aari.

'What do you want to know?' came the confident counter.

'That what progress you've made with Megha.' She was Aari's latest.

'First base,' was the prompt reply. The bluntness of Aari's response left Raghu totally clueless about his next recourse. All he could do was fumble.

'Uhh...I wasn't exactly talking about that kind of progress.'

'Is there any other kind?'

No answer was forthcoming. Finally, Abhay asked, 'How come just first base?' The scorn and sarcasm were camouflaged, save for the slightest twirl at the corner of his mouth.

'I guess she's too prim and propah,' replied an unfazed Aari 'Mark my words, boys. Never get involved with a Rapunzel who never lets her hair down. No way will you be able to make it into the castle.'

Even Abhay could not repress a smile. 'You're certainly not the picture of the regular IITian,' he said to Aari.

'I'm sure you mean that as a compliment. But alas, I cannot consider it so,' said Aari with the mock expression of a martyr.

'And why?' asked Abhay.

It was a while before Aari spoke.

'Because it has been made clear to me that this place is supreme,' he answered, all of a sudden becoming serious and caustic. 'And that IITians are a cut above the rest. They are the crème de la crème—as the French say—whereas all others are simply the common masses, the rabble, the proletariat, hoi polloi; children of a lesser God, if I may say so.'

An awkward silence followed. It then came to be known that Aari had an illustrious elder brother who had topped his batch during his stint in IIT. He was presently a research scientist with Bell Labs. Aari's parents absolutely doted and drooled upon him. As a result, Aari had no option but to follow him into IIT.

'Sometimes...' mumbled Raghu. He wanted to say something to ease the situation, but couldn't adequately figure out what.

Abhay, as dignity demanded, kept out of it.

The onus now lay upon Abeer. He could either meet the frayed nerves head-on, or he could fly off on a tangent. Abeer chose the former. 'I bet your brother is nowhere as street-smart and extroverted as you are. Keeps to his books and is quite uncomfortable among people,' said he after some thought.

'That's right,' agreed a surprised Aari. 'But how'd you know?'

'When parents favor one offspring, it's usually the one who *they* think is less equipped to cope with the world. That street-smart thing was just a guess. One of the things an IIT topper is likely to lag in.'

Aari became quiet, as if atoning for all his extroversion.

'But suppose there was no brother, what would you have chosen to become?' inquired Abeer, mainly to ease the silence.

'A writer,' blurted out Aari with passion. Then suddenly realizing that he was not acting his image, and the others would suspect that he was unable to handle his alcohol, jested, 'With my perpetual interest in other people's affairs, I guess there's no better career option. Not to mention the excuse this profession provides for sporting long hair.'

Everyone laughed. Less at the quip, and more to make him feel comfortable. It soon became evident that Aari would not stay long, and that he was essentially waiting for that first chance which wouldn't make his exit seem abrupt. Indeed, such a chance did not take long to arrive.

'I'll bestow you guys some time amongst yourselves,' said Aari as he shook hands with Abhay. It was palpable: the effort he was putting in to make everything seem jocularly pompous. 'Thanks to you, purveyor of good spirits, I now know a lot more about your two friends. Didn't realise co-inebriation could be so insightful.'

'Don't ever let that notion fool you,' replied Abhay good humouredly in the same affected vein as Aari's, 'But if you're so intent in employing a vice to delve into characters of fellow men, try gambling.'

'You can wager your donkey, that is, bet your ass I'll give that a try,' retorted Aari before he finally left. He liked to have the last word.

'It's just as well that your friend didn't get to be a writer,' remarked Abhay after a brief silence.

'Don't be so harsh,' objected Raghu, 'He's actually quite articulate.'

'*And* explicit.'

'What's wrong with explicit?'

'Apparently everything. Because the moment a thing

becomes explicit, it ceases to be profound. Be it art, literature, or cinema; it is only the implied and open ended which has reigned supreme. Why, even the genius of Aldous Huxley has been called *raw and uncooked* by Virginia Woolf. The message is clear and unequivocal: All you creative creatures out there, communicate in labyrinthine parables. You ask why? Well how else will you cater to people's vanity? Content which is understood clearly and understood by one and all will never elevate its patrons to their desired domain of exclusivity. Likewise, an idea that's pregnant with only a single categorical connotation can never be considered profound. So you see, it's the seductresses in an author which never allows her to drop that last bit of clothing.'

Silence. Then Raghu spoke unexpectedly, 'Do you remember the time when Shah had deliberately dropped his towel.'

'Ya. Pikku (the housemaster) was at the change-room gate. Shah had no other way to ward off his attention from the magazine.'

'The ploy had succeeded. Shah's *magazine*, as you call it, was salvaged.'

'Poor Pikku. Better nudes were not his lot.'

The conversation thus drifted to their days in Scad. Common memories were fished out from waters that had long passed under the bridge. Tingly and intoxicating, the memories were like wine. Time had weeded out from them such traces of bitterness which might have once existed. A couple of years from now, they would remember the current ordinary evening with the same relish.

It was about two in the morning when Abhay finally looked at his watch. The fishes had become scarcer and the silences longer. They finally decided to call it a day. Typical of Abhay, the farewell was an unostentatious one.

When the rear lights of Abhay's car had merged into the

night, Raghu spoke, 'I wonder how he's really faring.' Abhay had hardly spoken about his business during the course of the evening, and queries arising out of Raghu's genuine concern had been politely laughed off.

'Don't worry, Abhay being Abhay, he'll be okay,' assured Abeer.

'I think you're right. I mean, he's basically bright, he's good at managing stuff, and most important of all, he naturally elicits trust from people.'

'No. Most important of all would be the fact that he's an innately fair person. In a world where reputations travel fast, that translates into the highest commercial wisdom.'

'I guess it does. And who knows, he might already be doing pretty well. He looked reasonably pleased today.'

'Well *that* I guess was for a different reason.'

'What?'

'I think it was after a very long time that he got to be his own age. If only for a few hours.'

Bridal train of thought

The academic year had eventually drawn to its end. It was time for Lila to graduate. Not having gotten through to any of the top business schools, she intended to take up a soft job while she simultaneously prepared for B-school entrance once again. The original idea was for the job to be in Delhi but that plan had been thwarted by her father. 'If the job is mainly to embellish your CV, I see no reason why it can't be in Lucknow. Don't deprive your old man of your company. As it is, you have limited days left in his house.' Put that way, the logic was unassailable. Lila succumbed to it even though she was fully aware of the leash that such an arrangement would have on her love life. Her old man wasn't exactly the boyfriend-friendly sort.

'You might as well have been a CIA agent, and I one of your project-specific unofficial recruits,' said Raghu to Lila as they walked down platform number five at New Delhi railway station. He had come to see her off and the reference was to the first movie they had watched together.

Lila managed a mirthless laugh and Raghu continued in a mock dramatic voice, 'Don't contact us, we'll contact you. You'll be told everything on a need to know basis.' Lila laughed some more as Raghu went on, this time in his own voice 'Hell! I'm not allowed to ring you up. I'm not allowed to write to you.

What do I do? Take up a summer course in telepathy?'

'I'd rather you take heart. Haven't you heard, absence makes the heart grow fonder,' consoled Lila.

'Ab's sense is nothing but misplaced gut-feel. I'll any day prefer common sense to Ab's. And common sense dictates that we have some definite mode of communication.'

'That we will. Trust me, I'll soon find a way out.'

'That's what you've been telling me for the whole of last month.'

'It takes time, Raghu. Besides, I wasn't prepared for this situation. I hadn't at all expected that I won't make the cut.'

'Hadn't you? With your undying love for Maths!' Though he knew he shouldn't have said that, he didn't bother to apologize. He was too perturbed to do so. Luckily, Lila was understanding enough to let it go.

'I promise I'll come up with a solution,' she assured. 'Just give me some time. It's not that easy you know. We're pitted against my father—a rare specimen of the old school.'

'I don't give a damn what school he went to. But whichever it was, I'm sure it didn't prejudice its pupils against marrying off their daughters.'

'No prejudice against marrying them off. But yes prejudice against them choosing their own grooms.'

'C'mon, what hassles could your dad have with me? I'm a pretty conventional kind of guy. I mean, as conventional as you can expect them nowadays. Isn't it enough that I'm not the startling sort like Aari?'

'You don't get it. It's not about you. Even by dad's own yardstick, you're better than the guys he could hope to round up for me. Your only fault is that you haven't come to him through the traditional channels.'

A rather rancid remark brewed on Raghu's tongue. But as it chiefly featured her dad, he refrained from airing it. After all, there are limits to the liberties that can be availed of, even under the pretext of being perturbed. 'And what exactly would your dad mean by traditional channels?' he finally asked, after carefully stripping his query of all perilous accompaniments.

'A formal proposal, for one.'

'I could do that. Or get that done by my parents. Whichever your dad prefers.'

'There's a catch. The proposal needs a recommendation from a friend or relative. Friend needs to be close. Relative could be distant. Even a niece of the daughter-in-law of the first cousin of an aunt would work.'

'How the hell am I supposed to manage that?' asked Raghu irritably.

'You won't have to. Because dad will eventually realize how dried-up these channels of recommendation have become.'

Raghu's expression indicated that he considered such a change of heart very unlikely.

'The truth is that these long-chain recommendations—these devices which have been the mainstay of our traditional matchmaking—are now disappearing faster than the Indian tiger,' began Lila. 'Individual tolerance levels are decreasing by the day and divorce is no longer the taboo it used to be. Consequently, more and more marriages are falling apart. Now who in his right mind would want to propose candidates for such failure-prone ventures? You see, nobody wants to hear his own name as answer to the question "Whose suggestion was that rogue of a groom?" And the fact is that such questions are asked aplenty at family get-togethers. Asked for years together and asked especially when all assembled know the answer.'

Raghu smiled. Lila went on, as if engrossing a child with a story.

'Now we're not a society that provides conducive milieus for dating and mingling. At least not to the majority of us. So with the recommendation channel all dried up, middle class India has moved on to the next available option—the matrimonials. But fortunately, matrimonials have a drawback too.'

'What?' asked Raghu impatiently. He liked what he was hearing.

'Do your parents know that you smoke?' she asked abruptly.

'Yes they do. What's that got to do with it?'

'You'll soon see. Now tell me, do you ever smoke in their presence?'

'Never.'

'Or in the presence of their friends and acquaintances?'

'Not if I can help it.'

'Ever wondered why?'

'Umm…'

'I'll tell you. Though many people might call it hypocrisy, *we* refer to it as regard and consideration. R&C. As a society, we thrive on it. R&C is what prevents your father from saying no to the neighbor when he asks to borrow his car; and R&C is what prevented your Chacha from roughing you up when you slapped his son as a teenager. In short, R&C is the cement which binds up the *mohalla* and keeps the great Indian joint family together. But coming back to the topic at hand, it's what helps keep marriages together. Unfortunately, it's a commodity fast going out of fashion.'

Not quite able to follow her drift, Raghu looked at her blankly. Lila gauged his expression and began afresh. 'See, the dismal state of our manners—that is, the way we treat strangers whom we're unlikely to meet again—clearly shows that we don't proffer R&C to every Tom, Dick and Harry. Hence to compensate for that, we overdo the R&C with people whom we know reasonably well.'

'And?' asked Raghu with affected patience.

'And one such recipient of R&C was the friend-relative matrix through which matrimonial alliances came through. So from the very start of their married life, traditionally wedded couples were under the assumed watch of the R&C gang.

'In contrast, because none of those middlemen are involved in a current-day marriage, the modern-day couple is all on its own.'

'So good riddance to bad rubbish. The way I see it, a large R&C gang simply translates into a large pain in the A.'

'Agreed. But again, the gang did achieve one good objective. It exercised a benevolent restraint on the couple. Due to its influence, the couple kept under wraps all the smoke and fire from its day-to-day squabbles. Kept it under wraps *despite* the family knowing and the acquaintances guessing. Much like your smoking.'

'You're telling me that the couple never let its discord out of the bedroom?'

'Borrowing your phrase—not if they could help it.'

'And what purpose did this throttling serve?'

'Most minor quarrels were thus throttled to death. This took care of those initial years that demand maximum adjustment.'

Raghu waited a while before finally declaring, 'For all the R&D you've put into this R&C thing, I still don't buy the theory.'

'Okay, look at it this way. Let's suppose that the person instrumental in consummating this particular match is the groom's aunt—someone who dotes on the groom and vice-versa. Also, this aunt is a close friend and neighbor of the bride's parents. The bride's childhood was spent listening to fairy tales at the aunt's knee and blah, blah, blah. Now since both the bride and the groom have a high amount of R&C for this aunt, we can be assured of one thing.'

'And that is?'

'That the aunt's presence at the back of their minds will play a certain restraining role on both of them; partly because they like and respect her, and partly because they're both ambassadors of their respective families to her. The bottomline is that both of them would go the extra mile to maintain their good impressions on the aunt. The fallout of this would be that their petty disagreements would now be less likely to get public; and hence less likely to spiral into ugliness.'

'Okay, to an extent you're right. But you talk of petty disagreements. What about the major ones?'

'With petty disagreements not being allowed to get out of control, that's half the battle won. You'd be surprised at the number of marriages that go sour because of the incremental accumulation of petty issues. As for the major incompatibility issues that you talk about, there's every chance the good aunt would have combed through those before she set up the match.'

'But what does all this have to do with matrimonials? You were talking about those, weren't you?'

'Matrimonials, Raghu,' said Lila with a pause, 'don't come with the benefit of these mediating aunts and acquaintances. They come devoid of R&C.' Then as if winding up all that she'd been muttering, Lila added 'So with one conventional channel dried up and the second rather risky, it shouldn't be difficult convincing my dad to come to terms with the times. Further, if one were to...RAGHU,' she shrieked, cutting her sentence short. 'Did you see what that guy just did?'

'Which guy?' he asked.

'The one who just went by.'

'What'd he do?'

'He whistled and winked at me.'

Raghu was at a loss of words. More significantly, he was at a loss of his wits. This was the first time he was encountering a situation of this kind. All he could do was peer in the direction of the accused and mumble incoherently. Lila, obviously, did not take kindly to this.

'I don't believe you're just standing there doing nothing!' she said with rancour.

'And I don't believe a sensible person like you is trying to make an issue out of it,' he countered, resuming some poise.

'Someone misbehaves with your girlfriend and you don't consider it an issue?'

'It *would've* been an issue if all this had happened at another place. And the perpetrator was another person. But how much gravity can you ascribe to the actions of a bum? Whistling at sundry females must be routine for him. I mean, as long as he doesn't try to get physical or something, you're better off letting such sleeping dogs lie.'

The art of counter attacking has a rule. The magnitude of the attack needs to be above a certain threshold limit. Anything less than that and the whole exercise turns counterproductive.

Raghu's verbosity made Lila all the more convinced of her stand. And though she chose to keep mum, the look in her eyes showed her displeasure clearly. Also, since silence rarely fails to accentuate accusations, Raghu eventually found himself in justification mode.

'Look, I didn't even need to actually fight him, if that's what you're insinuating. The junta would've gladly done that for us. You know how little it takes to unleash their righteous anger. They would've beaten your tormentor to pulp and I was not even required to move a muscle.'

'They atrophy on disuse—the muscles,' she said after some thought. 'Most of all that muscle called self-respect.'

No one said anything after that. No one could.

The silence was finally broken by the sound of a whistle. This time, it was the train's—an announcement of its impending departure. Raghu quietly picked up Lila's bag and helped her to her seat. He waited for her to settle into place and as soon as she'd done so, turned around and started to leave. His mumbled farewell diffused on the tongue and all that an astonished Lila could perceive was his awkward wave of two fingers. 'Raghu wait,' she called out after him. He let the plea go unheeded and kept walking. The next thing he heard was that familiar flutter of steps—the flutter which used to precede her voice on the phone. He stopped to turn around and Lila, who hadn't compensated her pace for this sudden halt, banged straight into him. To hug him hard was but a reflex action. He naturally followed suit. It might have been the unexpectedness of it all, or it could have been the realization that they didn't have a definite date for their next meeting, the hug ripened into a kiss.

Much as the movies would have us believe, fellow passengers never clap when they see two lovebirds come together in the cited manner. The majority look away either in embarrassment or with unconcern. Some of the elderly paint their faces with the 'what have the times come to' look. As for those in the same age range, they look on with a malicious stare that clearly says 'if the times *have* come to this, why not me'. Lila and Raghu were totally oblivious of such stares. They had thrown all R&C for fellow passengers out of the window. But unknown to the two, the window was that of a moving train, and it was only at the next stop that Raghu could alight. Not that he minded it. In love, going the extra mile is seldom a displeasure.

Matching wits

The summer vacation ended, much to Raghu's relief. Being back in Delhi was being back among friends. More importantly, it was being back in the same country as Lila. He now rated his chances of meeting her as considerably enhanced.

Lila had called him up a few times during the vacation. Her father, she had informed, was showing signs of warming up to her cloaked suggestions. Also, she thought her job to be satisfactory (no interesting male colleagues, he had ascertained) and was missing him badly. In a nutshell, all was well on the eastern front.

As for the IIT campus, Raghu found it caught in a frenzy due to the cricket world cup. When people were not eating, sleeping, drinking, and smoking cricket, they were playing and watching it. And while the playing had metastasized to all conceivable sites, the watching was confined to just one—the common-room. But what a sight to behold that site was! It is said that one goes to a stadium not to watch a match but to enjoy it. In the hostel common-room, one could amply do both.

The best bits however were the discussions that cropped up in the wake of every match. Everybody was a part of them and everybody was an expert; but obviously, only the most vociferous got heard.

Not surprising then that Aari was now imposing himself upon a small audience. He was waxing eloquent on Tendulkar's cover drives which had brought home the bacon in the last match. Having enlightened the audience about the art of immaculate footwork, he was just about to flit to the subject of backfoot innovation and momentum timing when a passerby interrupted.

'Sounds like I missed an interesting match. The way you describe it Aari, am really tempted to watch the next one. Then again, I wonder whether taking eight hours off would be worth it.' The chap who thus wondered aloud was Shamit Tandon—a final year student who had spent a substantial part of his youth in the institute library. And not all in vain! He was a department topper with a C.G.P.A. of over 9.9. Also, being a hot favourite with the faculty, he had ascertained for himself at least three recommendations from the most influential professors in his discipline. Tandon actually had the career of his choice literally waiting for him. Whiling away eight hours, which is the approximate duration of a cricket match, was a luxury he could easily allow for. There was no need for him to mention the time factor. And it appeared that the only reason he had done so was to induce guilt amongst the masses.

Naturally, the masses didn't take too well to that inflicted emotion. They instantly sought an outlet for its noxious by-products. But since Tandon—their tormentor—didn't easily provide for any such clasps, all they could do was seethe in frustration. And what further aggravated that frustration was the trademark glow on Tandon's face; the glow that comes from a conscience which has been conciliated in the library for a good three hours; the glow of post *mugga* euphoria.

Ultimately, it was Aari who took up the cudgels on behalf of the *junta*. 'Interesting question, Tandon,' he began '"Whether taking eight hours off would be worth it?" Let's see. On the debit side we have the classes that are to be missed. On the credit side we have a day of lazing. But mind you, it's not plain lazing. It's lazing with a sport that's known to elicit character. So not only do we have fun but the learning that you miss in class is also duly compensated. One-day cricket, you see, is replete with lessons for life. There's so much that's common between the two.

'In cricket, you have limited overs to play within; here, in life, you have limited years. There you have limited wickets at your disposal, here you have limited resources. Runs are the fun part. We all want as many and as much as possible. The art of living, then, comprises in getting the balance correct between your overs, wickets and runs. It comprises in knowing when to brazenly attack, when to lie low, when to innovate, when to play the conventional shots; when to let the ball just go by —"Let it be" as John Lennon said.

'Now look at yourself. If we were to consider your IIT tenure as a fifty-over match, this is where you stand: Thirty-eight overs gone by, all ten wickets intact. And what do you do? Contend yourself with stealing ones and twos. *Ab to maaro, yaar*. Go for the long handle. Step out of the crease and loft those Tuesday classes over the boundary.'

Those assembled, laughed. More at Tandon than at the barb. It was understandable. Most of them were in their twenty-sixth over with seven wickets already down.

Amid the laughter, Aari pulled Tandon aside and added as an afterthought 'You know it Tandon, none of us intends to stay in the country. So why not enjoy these remaining moments of collective patriotism?'

Tandon kept looking at him fixedly with a bemused smile. Finally, he spoke, 'But of course, sports and national pride! I'm sorry the connection between the two didn't occur to me on its own. But then, it's not such an innately obvious connection, you see. Not all of us hinge national pride upon the fortunes of a bunch of bat-wielders and orb-hurlers.' There was a brief pause before he continued, 'Tell you what Aari, I think I'll give the Tuesday match a miss after all. But should India beat Pakistan that day, I'll definitely accompany all of you to the Wagah border. God! What fun we'll have sticking out our tongues to those Pakis on the other side!'

There was a stunned silence. Then very reluctantly, Aari conceded a smile. He had seen Tendulkar do the same when beaten by an Akram yorker.

Love and MA 120

'B-13 Raghu Kumar, B-13 Raghu Kumar,' shouted the security guard to inform Raghu about his call on hold on the hostel telephone. Raghu's heart pounded. Experience from the past four months told him that the call was Lila's. This was about the hour she usually rung up.

He picked up the receiver and found it cold against his ears. Winter had begun to set-in and the temperature looked poised to make a sudden plunge.

'I'm getting married, Raghu,' she abruptly announced.

Raghu convinced himself he hadn't heard that.

'I'm getting married, Raghu,' she repeated. 'Have been meaning to tell you. Just couldn't muster up the courage when we got talking.'

Raghu went numb. There was no initial pain. Nature, it is said, has a similar provision in place for great physical injuries as well.

He barely heard what Lila went on to say. It was something about her dad pressuring her into an early marriage on account of his ill health. The MBA, she explained, had just been her ploy to buy time for him to graduate and get a job. Her getting into a top B–school would have caused her dad to succumb to her allegedly bright career prospects. He would then put aside concerns about her marriage. However, even five full months of dedicated preparation had failed to enhance her mock test results. The MBA didn't look to happen.

As sensation eventually began to return, Raghu realized that he was required to say something. He would not have it that the last picture she carried of him would be that of a broken weakling.

'What does he do?' he at last managed to utter. He deliberately did not ask for the name. Hearing her pronounce it could well have been the last straw.

'He's an industrialist,' she replied, almost in a whisper.

'How long have you being seeing each other?'

'About a month.'

'And you...' he started, and stopped. The question was futile.

There was a brief silence before he spoke again. 'Tell me, would things have been different if I'd bashed up that bum at the station?'

'Raghu please...'

He cut her short. 'Be sure you train your industrialist for it.'

Pain rarely brings out the best in people—at least not at its very onset. As if it were a sea being churned, it first lets surface all that which is base and ugly. The treasures follow only later.

'Do try to understand Raghu...'she began. What followed was the standard bunch of rehearsed sentences conjoined in an incoherent manner. And it was in the middle of that soliloquy that he placed the receiver on the cradle. At that time, this seemed like an honorable exit.

Raghu stood staring at the cold dead receiver and it gradually dawned upon him why all matters of the heart were attributed to that organ. The throbbing heaviness in the left side of his chest was no psychosomatic sensation. It was very much for real. And for real too were the uninvited tears that presently arrived—at first in pairs, and then abandoning all such propriety, in torrents. As he made those quick strides to get away from it all, he found himself choked for air. He was nearly sobbing when Abeer saw him enter their room.

Very few people know how to handle a sobbing grown up male. Abeer wasn't one of them. He kept to his side of the room and waited. And when he had waited for what he thought was long enough, he very cautiously posed the question, 'Lila?'

'Just leave me alone,' was the reply.

'She getting married?' Abeer had somehow guessed this outcome some time back.

The silence which followed confirmed the conjecture and Abeer at once knew that it was time for pre-emptive action. Being an admirer of Louis Pasteur's germ theory, his first priority was to secure the fresh open wound from prevailing infections. He soon stood knocking outside Aari's door.

'Open locks, whoever knocks. No one here, shakes-the-spear,' came the assurance from inside, which is so necessary in a boys' hostel.

Abeer went in and was surprised to see Aari engrossed with a course textbook.

'MA 120,' was Aari's explanation to Abeer's raised eyebrows, 'Maths at its ball breaking best.'

'It *is* a bit difficult,' conceded Abeer.

'Bit difficult!' echoed Aari, 'Did they in Scad allow you to be that sloppy with your adjectives? My arse, bit difficult! Well I'll tell you what's made it a bit *more* difficult. Ramaswami—the course coordinator this semester. The chap thrives on Fs. He has the devil's curse. He can't orgasm until he's flunked at least fifteen chaps in a course. And you know what? I can't shake off this dirty feeling that I'm gonna make it to the chosen fifteen of that pageant.'

'The reason I'm here Aari,' began Abeer after clearing his throat, 'is to let you know that Lila has called it off. She's probably getting married to someone else. Raghu, as expected, isn't taking it well. I suggest that you be as discreet as possible when you talk to him. In case you can, avoid him altogether for the next couple of days.'

'Man! *This* is the time she chooses to pull the plug on him? With the MA120 major tomorrow and Ramaswami all oiled up? Tell you what, I'd sensed this all along. I mean, how much acumen can you expect from a girl who hasn't got sense enough to know her right cup size. Didn't you notice, the cleavage was never in proportion to the size of her...'

'Aari...Aari,' Abeer cut him short. He wanted to say something severe but contended himself with a mild reprimand. 'You really ought to abandon that single-track thought process. You can't breeze through life holding those kind of beliefs.'

'Holding what kind of beliefs?' asked Aari.

'That all there is to women are breasts.'

'You know Abeer,' mimicked Aari with a grin, 'I'll breeze through life believing exactly that. And a life of philanthropy it's going to be too. It's going to be a life lived for udders. And mind you, if I do end up having my way, women will forever be unshackled from the plight where men look at their faces when they talk to them.'

Despite his solemn mood, Abeer could not suppress a smile. He shook his head at the incorrigible Aari and started to walk out of the room. It was just as well that he had made this visit, he said to himself. There was no limit to the damage which Aari could have wreaked.

Just as he was about to shut the door to his room, Abeer heard Aari muttering to himself, 'Too much for a guy to take. Failing in love and MA120 in the same week!'

Love and MA120! The phrase had an interesting ring to it. And as he turned it around in his head for consideration, Abeer was suddenly struck by an inspiring thought. Of course, Love and MA120! Given Raghu's impatient and brooding nature, it was evident that 'time' was going to be a messy healer. The matter needed to be tackled in precise, objective and logical steps; it needed to be tackled here and now. Yes, it had to be Love and MA120.

Three days had passed since the phone call and Raghu's mess-boycott program had started to ebb. He had now begun to endure the basic calorie intake. Also, there had been some abatement in the 'morning sickness' which accompanies such grief—the sickness wherein one wakes up in the morning and the first few minutes are spent in the hope that the prevailing mess is just a bad dream. Then reality dawns anew. And because it is anew, it blows away all dust that had settled upon the grief during the course of the previous day. Sickening indeed!

Abeer decided that the time was ripe. He walked up to Raghu's side of the room and found him lying in bed, staring at the ceiling.

'Want to talk about it?' asked Abeer softly.

Raghu didn't reply.

Abeer waited a while before he started, 'You see Raghu, all this...'

'Abeer,' Raghu cut him short, 'Thanks...but...I already know all that crap about time being the great healer and all happening for the best and...I'll find someone better...Just let it be.'

'Those are precisely the things I was not going to say. I was here to play the mathematical shrink,' smiled Abeer.

Raghu couldn't help peering at what lay beyond that soft smile. Here was one person, he said to himself, whose allegiance, integrity and selflessness he could never doubt. Here was someone who had always been there for him. And he was there for him now; offering assistance and yet employing the tact and caution which befitted a supplicant. How could Raghu even think of snubbing him!

If only for a short while, grief had to be relegated to the back-burner. Raghu pushed his pillow against the wall as he began to prop himself up.

'What happened?' asked Abeer.

'If you're going to play shrink, I'd better get into the right position.'

'And also the right inclination, if possible' added Abeer.

A smile almost sprouted but Raghu quashed it in the nick of time. He would have quashed it even if Abeer hadn't been present. Self-pity has its rules.

'Knowing your patience, I'll get to the point straight away,' began Abeer. 'Let me start by listing the reasons behind your supposed pain.'

'Supposed, you say.'

'Sorry, wrong choice of word. What I meant was...'

'Go on,' interrupted Raghu, 'Tell me about the reason behind my pain.'

'Not reason; reasons. Plural. There are three of them you see. The first: Anger at her betrayal. In other words, a beating to your self worth. The second: Realization of the loss—the apprehension that something such will never be yours again. And the third: Jealousy—visions of her having a good time with someone else.'

'That *does* about cover the gamut, doesn't it?' said Raghu acerbically.

'Let's take up reason number one. Betrayal. In more honest words, rejection. And since rejection is directly hinged to our self worth, it obviously deals a pretty severe blow; unless of course we're able to better comprehend the basics behind its working.

'As far as your case goes, I can say with conviction that rejection did not come on its own. She was pressured into it. Nevertheless, we'll not seek refuge in that sort of rationalization. We'll assume the worst case scenario. We'll assume that she rejected you outright and that she did so because she didn't find you worthwhile. Now, the question that begs our attention is: what is this "you" that she rejected?'

'Might as well tell me.' The mild sarcasm sprang from the desire to appear strong and composed.

'The "you" my friend is a package. It's a package called Raghu Kumar. It's attributed with a certain physique, certain voice, certain facial features, certain IQ, and a certain knowledge base. It brings along a certain financial security. It has a certain sense of humour, a certain generosity, a certain honesty. It has certain social, financial and managerial skills. It reacts to certain situations in certain ways. And based, or not based on the above, it has a certain market value'

'Of course, that's all that I am.'

'To yourself, you could be a lot more. But to the outside world, that's about what you are. People befriend you, hire you, and love you because of the package that you are. The true acceptance thing comes in much later, if at all.'

'I thought you were here to cheer me up.'

'I am. That in fact is a salient feature of the package called Abeer. Anyway, coming back to the rejection thing, I think there are three basic reasons why someone rejects a package. One, the rejecter has not been able to assess the package qualities in full. Two, she has assessed the qualities in full, but decides that those qualities are not in keeping with *her* priorities. Three, she has assessed the qualities in full, they are in keeping with her priorities, but...but she's found a package that offers more. Well if it's case one and two, good riddance of bad rubbish. You don't want to spend your life with someone who doesn't acknowledge or appreciate the package that you are. You'll find lots of others who do.'

'What if it's case three?' asked Raghu, not without trepidation.

'In that case, welcome to the real world. He who lives by the sword must die by the sword.'

'What do you mean live and die by the sword?'

'You know that short girl from textile who's always making eyes at you?' asked Abeer.

'The one with a nasty scar on her chin?'

'Alas! You deliver another. She falls prey to the sword yet again.'

'Abeer the bastard! You don't expect me to settle for her.'

'And why not? Because she's not much to look at? She's certainly intelligent. And she could have a heart of 24K gold for all you know. Isn't that what you lovebirds lay a heavy premium on?' demanded Abeer.

Raghu didn't reply and Abeer continued, 'When a woman gives importance to a guy's financial status while appraising him, we call her shallow. But it's all right when *we* evaluate women on the basis of an attribute that's only skin deep!'

Raghu's embarrassment was evident. He scurried to get the

conversation into more generic realm. 'So what you're essentially telling me is that it's okay to flit from package to better package,' he said.

'I'm not saying it's okay to flit, I'm only saying its natural. Because ideally, the flitting should stop once a commitment has been made. But again, the definition of commitment varies from person to person. For some it's a word. For others it's marriage. And there are those who don't consider four mutual kids as commitment enough. However, that's not what we're discussing. The point I'm trying to make is that all of us have a fixed concept of ourselves, the "I". Each of us instinctively knows that there's something to "I" which is greater than the sum total of the package's attributes. In fact, the "I" may even be totally different from the mosaic of attributes. In a nutshell, the "I" is what defines us to ourselves, much like the package is what defines us to the outside world. The "I" is therefore far more vulnerable than the package. Hence, when a rejection comes along, the first thing you need to do is to segregate the "I" from the mess. You need to guard it from assaults which aren't meant for it. And, should your "I" get hit even after all your precautions, you need to pamper it. You need to indulge it with anything that makes it feel good about itself. Remember, most misery and rebound-relationships are the result of a wounded "I".

'So when dealing with any kind of failure or rejection, try and keep your "I", your self-worth, intact. Realize that what's gone wrong are mere circumstances; what's taken the beating is the package—the market contingent entity. Duly ensure that that beating doesn't affect you. Alternatively, if you happen to be one of those who identify too much with the package, that market-contingent entity…'

'Then?' interrupted Raghu impatiently.

'Well then you'd need to play by the market rules. You'd need to accept, adapt, or upgrade.'

There was silence for a while.

'Since my client is still in the seat and I'm being paid by the hour, might as well make the best of it. Second point. Realization of the loss. Apprehension that something such will never be yours again.'

Raghu gave a weary look. And Abeer at once knew he wanted to listen on.

'First question. Who, according to you, were you in love with?' Abeer asked.

'Let me guess. I was not in love with her but a package that was her, which in fact was the alter ego of the package that was her mother,' answered Raghu derisively.

Abeer laughed. 'Nice to see the sensahuma back. But actually, it's far simpler than that. You Raghu were in love with what you imagined her to be. Not what she was.'

'Bullshit.'

'Is it? You fall in love with the first girl who comes your way and she has all those qualities that you ever wanted in a woman. Now isn't that stretching the laws of probability a bit too far? Woe to thee Einstein! God *does* play dice.'

'Okay. So she might have been acting a bit better than her usual self. One does that when in love,' countered Raghu.

'Wrong, once again. One doesn't *act* good when in love, one simply *is*. Blame it on the intoxicating effect of that chemical mix—dopamine, serotonin, oxytocin, etc, etc. Do you remember that incident with Gupta last semester? He was trying so hard to bait you into a spat. You were so benign and understanding. And with Gupta! The chap you can't stand. Now if being in love can make Gupta seem tolerable, imagine what it can make the person you're in love with.

'Or look at it this way. One, she's a reasonably good person to begin with. Two, her being in love makes her an even better person. Three, your being in love with her makes her seem even, even better. Four, your combined trances makes you believe anything about each other that you might want to.'

'So three magnifying glasses in all!'

'All strategically positioned and all heavy distorters. The final projection was nothing like what was placed under the scanner. You simply took hold of a personality that came your way and filled in the blanks by yourself. Trust me, the person you've lost is nowhere close to the person you *imagine* you've lost. The real damage is far less. And a replacement will not at all be difficult to come by,' concluded Abeer.

'Now that last thing you said sounds nothing like you. It's got Aari written all over it. Man, the chap's contagious,' put in Raghu.

Abeer smiled, 'Which reminds me. I have to be going. Aari and I are trying out this new eating joint in Saket. Care to join?'

'No. But aren't you going to finish off with that jealousy thing?' blurted out Raghu, a bit too impatiently.

'Got you!' laughed Abeer. 'Though your weary faces were a giveaway too.'

'Aari *is* contagious,' reiterated Raghu.

'The jealousy thing,' continued Abeer, not wanting to stretch the joke any further, 'is the trickiest of the three, and is in fact the most difficult to deal with. Jealousy warps emotions to an extent that you could actually accuse it of *creating* new ones. "It was jealousy which made him imagine that he loved Semira." The "him" of course is Voltaire's Zadig. And Semira, I think, is symbolic of not just a woman but of almost any desirable object.'

Raghu couldn't care less what Semira was symbolic of. All that mattered was Lila. And now that Abeer had articulated the potency of jealousy, what had with great difficulty been reduced to a nebulous throb once again became a full blown pang.

'She's seeing somebody else,' said Raghu, vocalizing the pang.

'She's gone, Raghu,' said Abeer at length, 'Why should it matter whether she's having a blast or is pining for you? She emerged from the crowd and into the crowd she has once again melted. You don't bother about others in the crowd. So why should it matter whether *she* is lonesome or is being wooed by dozens? None of those scenarios affect your reality.'

'They bloody well *do*,' contested Raghu.

'No they don't. All they affect is your petty ego,' countered Abeer almost immediately. Almost immediately too, he regretted having said that. It was some time before he could speak again.

'When we look at breakups Raghu, it always seems that one party is taking it better than the other. But have you ever wondered why it's that way?'

'It's because one of the parties is a hard-hearted bitch.'

'No,' laughed Abeer softly, 'it's that way because that party saw it coming. It saw the breakup coming a bit earlier than the other party did. The pain therefore got spread out over a bigger duration of time. So when you compare your pain to Lila's, you're in effect comparing her "installment" with your "down payment". The former is bound to be lesser. And c'mon, even for the most hardened of what you call a bitch, a breakup would be heart-wrenching. I'm sure it wouldn't be her idea of fun.

'Come to think of it, this whole breakup thing is so much like a road accident. It's unfortunate, it's avoidable, and it's futile trying to figure out whose fault it was. And even though the more vulnerable party incurs heavier losses, that doesn't imply that the less vulnerable one wanted the accident to happen.'

'So?' asked a defiant Raghu.

'So just because she's seeing somebody doesn't mean she's better off than you are. All she's trying to do is pick up the pieces and move on. Trust me, her smile is nothing but a brave attempt at camouflage. Don't grudge her that smile. It is with some effort that it makes it to her lips.'

Raghu's upturned gaze seemed as if it would never let go of the ceiling. Then all of a sudden, he broke out into a queer smile.

'What?' asked Abeer.

'Nothing,' said Raghu. 'Was just reminded of your first evening in Scad. You mouthing away all kinds of incongruent stuff; me taking you to be an adorable idiot, only to later realize that you were perhaps the sanest person there.'

'So…'

'So I so much hope this is a repeat performance.'

Abeer burst into a laugh, amid which, Raghu inquired, 'Can I ask you something?'

'Of course,' answered Abeer

'What did you tell Aari about this whole thing?'

'How'd you know I told him?' retorted Abeer.

'He's been giving me the look that one reserves for a puppy with a broken paw, though in Aari's case, I'm not sure if puppies actually elicit that look.'

'The look's because he thinks you're going to flunk in MA120,' explained Abeer.

'I'm not. I did okay,' said Raghu with just the hint of some pride.

'I'd thought as much. Vulnerability alongside resilience! Such an adorable Indian trait. By the way, please excuse me for breaking a promise I'd made earlier.'

'Which one?'

'That I won't talk about you finding someone better and...'

'Go on.'

'You know, I'm so sure that you will. And very soon too,' assured Abeer with all the conviction at his disposal.

Raghu looked away, all of a sudden feeling wistful.

'I'm sorry...' said Abeer.

'It's not you. I was reminded of something similar she'd said before signing off.'

'What? If I may ask.'

'That broken hearts are fertile grounds,' he let out reluctantly in a whisper. The possibility of a lurking Aari couldn't entirely be ruled out.

Part III

Neti neti (Not this, not this)

The Chinese had declared it to be the year of the dog, and a carefree gaggle of young boys had turned into a dour drift of middle-aged men.

Abhay had taken his business from strength to strength—much as Raghu and Abeer had anticipated that drunken night—and his company was now a fairly respected scrip at the stock exchange. In the meanwhile, he had also found time to get married. Tania was her name.

Abeer was stationed in Niranjanpur—a small town in Himachal. His work was what he was wedded to.

Aari, who had moved to the US after graduation, had struck gold with a dot-com startup. He cashed out at an opportune time and was now an angel investor. Since the aversion he had for routines extended to relationship commitments as well, he was still a bachelor. To him, a woman was either a wondrous thought or a tiresome problem. And he always found it convenient to sleep with such predicaments before deciding on any subsequent action.

Raghu, after securing an MBA degree from IIM Calcutta, had joined a reputed business house. He had since hopped a couple of jobs; a few times for latitude and at others for altitude. Once, for plain attitude. For his age and qualifications, he was doing better than okay and was presently heading sales in a pharmaceutical firm of some standing. Abeer's prophesy—about him meeting someone—had eventually turned out to be true. Raghu's colleague from one of his jobs was his wife now. They also had a daughter: Vini.

And it was to Vini's prospective school that Raghu and Nandini were now headed.

'Can you figure out why a second interview for a nursery admission?' demanded an unreasonable and exasperated Raghu. He had had to miss an allegedly important meeting at work.

Nandini had been with him long enough to know the question to be a rhetorical one. She didn't bother to reply. Beatles on the car audio kept ranting about it being a hard day's night.

Raghu reached out for his cigarette packet, then spotting Vini in the rear view mirror, decided against it.

'Tense?' asked Nandini.

'Who wouldn't be? Have you gone through this admission form? The guys want to know what our family philosophy is! Hell, are families supposed to have a categorically delineated philosophy? I tell you, even fiction writers would have problems completing this form.'

Nandini laughed. One of those small mechanical laughs that couples of five years and above reserve for use with one another.

And though Raghu was well versed with the connotation of that laugh, he shamelessly chose to avail of it at face value. He duly laughed back. This was to be the worm hole that would transport him to a conversational universe which he hadn't been able to access since morning. Curiously, it was this dread of access which was the real reason behind his looming exasperation. 'Forgot to tell you,' he started matter-of-factly, 'Was talking to Abhay in the morning. Have invited him for dinner tomorrow.' Nandini shot a sharp look at him. She was not particularly fond of Abhay. Even less of his wife Tania.

It was a prolonged silence after which she inquired 'Along with his wife?' The coldness in her voice could have frozen a volcano on Mercury.

'No, just him.'

'Thank God,' she remarked, and after a pause, added abruptly, 'With what they mean to each other, I don't understand the delay in divorce.'

'Do you really have to use that word in the child's presence?' blurted Raghu. The anger ran more in the tone of his voice than in its volume. Because even though the bottled up exasperation had found a legitimate exit, it was in no position to completely abandon prudence.

'She's just four!' countered Nandini.

'More the reason. Why let those negative emotions take seat in her tender mind? And mind you, words do that.'

'You're right,' said Nandini sarcastically. 'If we don't use that word, she'll never come to know of it.'

'She's also going to learn cursing at some point. Might as well start exposing her to that.'

The brief silence that ensued was broken by Nandini.

'You still haven't answered my question.'

Obviously, the answer to the question held little importance for her. She was just pressing the point because she was annoyed with the prospect of an evening with Abhay. Not to mention, the reprimand just received in the presence of a four year old.

'Which was?'

'Why don't they seek a divorce?'

'Because it doesn't matter,' said Raghu flatly.

'It doesn't matter!' repeated Nandini, meticulously separating each word. 'And these are the kind of best friends you have!'

It was in a mock baritone that she continued, 'Would you like some cream with your coffee? Uhh...no, I think I'll have a divorce instead. On second thoughts, let it be. It doesn't matter.'

'You wouldn't understand,' said an irritated Raghu.

'Of course I wouldn't. I'm not from the I...I...M.'

'You wouldn't understand because you haven't known Abhay for the last twenty-five years.'

'Six is long enough, thank you.'

They had reached Vini's school. Raghu closed his eyes as he shut off the ignition, then taking a deep breath, turned to Nandini.

'Why are we doing this? Okay, I'm touchy because Kalra is going to create a lot of shit behind my back in that meeting I'm missing. You on your part are not exactly glad that Abhay's coming over. But c'mon, this is about our daughter's first step into the outside world.'

Nandini's solemn expression was her way of saying that she agreed. The two had bought some temporary peace.

Raghu scanned a newspaper and Kalra—the chief finance officer from his firm—tinkered with his cell-phone as they whiled away time at an upmarket café. They were waiting for Monty Kapoor to arrive. Monty was the scion of their company's promoter family. He was also the reason that this waiting was being done in a café and not a boardroom. Monty believed that important meetings with important employees needed to be conducted in informal settings. Monty also believed in never turning up for such meetings on time, for what was punctuality if not a plebian affliction. Actually, Monty believed in a lot of things; and prime amongst such things was *insaaniyat* (loose translation: humanity.) Monty considered himself to be a champion of this cause. Out of the various ways in which he attended to it, his favourite was discussing employee welfare schemes with top management. Of course, he was astute enough to calibrate dosage in accordance with the candidate's personality.

At the bottom of the rung was the HR (Human Resources) head. And he was at the bottom for good reason. The man had a loathsome tendency of coming up with definite steps for an actual implementation of Monty's suggestions. Quite obviously, it was only rarely that Monty touched him on the subject. Next in line were Raghu and Karan Seth(the Chief Executive Officer). Though their performance was just about the satisfactory mark—a patient ear and an appreciatively nodding head was all they brought to the table—they made up for it by contributing towards variety, what every speaker seeks in his audience profile. And finally, positioned at the top of the mound, was the inimitable Ravi Kalra. The man whose initiative and enterprise were worthy of documentation. Kalra would patiently hear-out all of Monty's schemes and then come up with valid objections to them. He would apprise Monty of the pressing need of funds in areas vital to the company's—and therefore ultimately, the employees'—survival. Monty would then be left with no option but to abandon his proposed scheme. All in the name of *insaaniyat*.

Monty stormed into the café (his was the kind of personality that could only storm in, and never breeze by) and expressed regret at being late. The regret was expressed from a distance of three tables from where Raghu and Kalra were sitting, and the two of them were collectively referred to as 'my young vice presidents'. This was a subtle Monty (not for him the passé namedropping of being held up by a so-and-so) putting his identity in perspective to all and sundry. Indeed, all and sundry did take time off to steal a glance at him; and Monty swaggered to his table basking in, what he believed to be, their admiration.

He was about to take a seat but stopped himself in the nick of time. He had spotted something grossly disturbing in the seating arrangement. Theirs was a table with two chairs and two sofas, and since the sofas were already taken, Monty had been left with the unwelcome choice of just chairs. Not that he had anything against chairs, but these particular ones appeared to be somewhat lowly. More so when juxtaposed with the luxuriant sofas.

Monty's was a profound dilemma. He could either have the sofas vacated by hinting at his preference (and thus go against *insaniyat*), or he could altogether forego that seat of higher hierarchy. Foregoing was obviously not an option. What good was it to have a mind of one's own if one couldn't act out that mind's choices?

Luckily, a solution lurked in the neighborhood. Monty spotted a table of four where all four seats were sofas. Obviously, the fact that that table was already taken did not in any way seem like a hurdle to him. He peremptorily summoned a waiter and assigned him a task. The couple at the all-sofa table was to be requested to exchange their table with his. Interestingly, even though the waiter was astounded with this outrageous demand, he dutifully followed instructions. Such was the authority of Monty's demeanor! 'They're just two. Both of them will still get sofas here,' Monty explained to Raghu, and then went on to speculate, 'Let's see! If they're reasonable, they'll agree.'

Indeed, the young couple agreed; probably because they were in the flush of first love and were oozing the milk of human kindness, or probably because they were an exceptionally generous couple. Of course, it was also possible that they were—as Monty had speculated—plainly reasonable.

Monty proceeded to his rightful table while Raghu, seeing that his boss had failed to do the needful, scuttled to thank the young couple. Monty shook his head as he laughed and remarked to Kalra, 'These UK people are all the same. Jolly—my cousin brother who's settled there—also believes a lot in this thank-you *shank-you* business.' Monty was proud of his ability in spotting demographic trends.

Supper was ordered—with Monty picking some of the items and 'suggesting' the rest—even as the two vice-presidents braced themselves for the news that had necessitated this meeting. Monty didn't take long to arrive at the point. It turned out that the rumor in the office wasn't merely a rumor. Karan Seth was actually leaving. And since Monty believed in frankness (which was a term he often confused with rudeness), he personally wanted to inform both of them about the course that lay ahead. Depending upon their performance and their willingness to partially forego Seth's pay and perks ('given the difficult times the company is going through'), one of them could hope to be promoted to his position.

Luckily for the Kumars, Vini was granted admission in the school of their choice. And success being a good temporary antidote to acrimony, the mood in the Kumar household was now conducive enough to entertain guests. There was time for Abhay to arrive and Raghu was judiciously utilizing it to chat up Nandini.

'You were actually very good at the interview,' he prattled. Any damage by Kalra had been contained and the evening with Abhay held its promise. Not much more is required to turn on the tap of human goodness. 'Reminded me of our days in ICL. Those Machiavellian plots to get into the same project team, those packed dinners, late night coffees! Wasn't working together wonderful?'

His mood was enhanced by the situation. Though temporary, his happiness was by and large genuine.

'Don't have too much to drink, Raghu,' she replied, as she set the timer on the microwave. She always tested his patience before entering the kind of conversation he was now initiating.

'Of course not,' he retorted, 'Important meeting with the Zydus people tomorrow. Can't afford to be late.'

'You had an important meeting the next day when Abhay was here last time. It had gone unattended.'

'C'mon, that was a routine meeting,' he put in feebly; not as an excuse, but simply to keep the conversation rolling.

'Of course it was! In a perfect world, the importance of meetings is an adjustable feature.'

'What do you mean?' A hint of annoyance was beginning to show.

'What I mean is that when a meeting is missed because of a hangover, it's labeled routine. But when you miss one because you have to attend your daughter's admission interview, you use it as an excuse for being testy.'

The microwave beeped. But Raghu didn't explode, even though the accusation fulfilled the necessary condition of detonation—that of being on either extreme of the truth-lie spectrum.

He walked out of the kitchen and into the living room. Nandini followed him shortly. Having got to speak out her mind without him retaliating, it was only natural that she was in the white-flag mood now.

'You were talking about the joys of working together,' she offered.

Had Raghu continued this conversation in the same vein as he had originally started, it would perhaps have resulted in another make-up. But Raghu's intentions did not get to see the light of day, for presently the bell rang.

It was Abhay at the door and Nandini greeted him affably. After the exchange of usual pleasantries, she proposed to take leave on pretext of grocery shopping. She also put in something about having to thank Menaaz—her friend who'd been of help in Vini's admission.

No sooner had Nandini left than Raghu set out to complete a formality that she'd deliberately omitted.

'How is Tania?' he enquired.

'Self-obsessed. Like most beautiful women,' was the dry reply. And Raghu at once knew, from the tone of that answer, that there was some truth to the rumors which he had been hearing through the week. He had in fact intended to enquire about them during the course of the evening, but it now seemed imperative that that query be served up as first course.

'There is some talk I've been hearing,' he began nonchalantly, as he uncorked a bottle of Caol Ila.

'Ah, eighteen years!' remarked an observant Abhay, 'It's nice to see your alcohol aging along with you.'

'Unluckily, not all things improve with time. As I was saying, I've heard some talk...that...'

'That I intend to sell off my business.'

'Yes,' stammered Raghu, quite taken aback. It was only after a pause that he could ask whether that was true.

'No smoke without fire,' answered Abhay.

'You can't do this!' said Raghu excitedly.

'I didn't confirm that I was going to. But why do you say I *can't* do it?'

'For the simple reason that you've put so much into this. You've built this thing from a *lala* enterprise to a corporate entity.'

'Doesn't that give *me* the right to go ahead?'

They were thus far into the conversation when Raghu suddenly realized his folly. It was possible that Abhay actually didn't have the answers which Raghu was trying to exact. Perhaps, he hadn't as yet made up his mind and was here for that very purpose. Raghu changed gear.

'You have every right to fritter away that which you've earned. Which reminds me, when are we to expect the delivery of your Ferrari?'

Abhay smiled queerly.

'Don't tell me!' almost shrieked a disappointed Raghu.

Abhay gave a faint nod to confirm the conjecture.

'Wow!' continued Raghu with affected sarcasm. 'Now we have a monk who didn't even buy a Ferrari.'

Abhay smiled again, this time his usual one.

'I get it!' said Raghu shortly. 'It's that *bidi* baron from M.P.'

Recently, there had been an article in the papers about the plush lifestyles of some *bidi* barons. One of them was said to own a Ferrari. And since selling *bidis* was not considered socially at par with, say, selling steel or software, Raghu surmised that to be the reason behind the Ferrari's lost gleam.

'It's not the *bidi* baron,' said Abhay, truthfully. He was too proud for it to be the *bidi* baron. Not buying the Ferrari because of him would have been tantamount to according him a great deal of respect.

A silence followed, and despite there being graver issues at hand, Raghu couldn't help using it to ponder upon the Ferrari that almost was. So palpable was his disappointment that it eventually elicited some solace.

'No need to fret about it,' offered Abhay 'three months is the maximum it lasts.'

'The Ferrari?'

'The *kick* from the Ferrari,' he corrected, 'along with the kick from everything else that you call material success—the dream villa, getting listed on the national stock exchange, cornering the major market share, you name it.'

Raghu wondered whether Tania fitted into the same category.

'It's actually quite unlucky to never be unlucky,' continued Abhay. 'Life becomes a monotony of strive, achieve, strive, achieve…Striving is spent in anticipation of achieving. And the hangover of the achievement is never more than three months. Then it's back to square one. The whole thing's no different than the life of a drug addict. You subsist on these three month shots and progressively keep getting immune to the last dosage. And honestly, not everyone has the sagacity of an Edison to say that he hasn't failed; that he's in fact discovered tens of ways in which happiness eludes him.'

'If we could all have problems like yours,' put in Raghu. Never having been a witness to Abhay's outpourings, he was more than a little surprised. And scared. That was the reason he was taking refuge in frivolity.

Abhay let it go unheard and the torrent continued unabated. 'The thing's interesting only as long as the fight's for basic survival. But once that level's crossed, it turns into a game of glorified monopoly. You know, make-believe notes and plastic property.

'I don't know how many times I've wanted to pull out. But self doubt always creeps in. "Am I calling it quits because I find the game interesting no more; or am I doing so because I'm scared of losing to the big boys?" Hell! I don't even know why that doubt should be creeping in because the truth of the matter is that *now*, the game is only more lucid than it was at the grassroots. Yes, more nefarious at times, but so much more predictable. And so I play along, each time thinking that I'll quit at the next turn; that I'll quit when in sight of the leader, if not at that position. But come to think of it, what is a leader anyway? There have been many such before him and there'll be many more after him. I fail to see any exclusivity in that position.'

God, thought Raghu, what it must be to earn the right to that kind of conceit! 'This level you talk of—the level after which it was interesting no more—when was that?' he asked, even though he well knew that he was at no risk of breaching the said level. He had asked the question merely because politeness demanded that he say something.

'When there was enough for a dignified existence,' replied Abhay after some thought. It was a practical answer, and it also seemed to bring Abhay back to the practical world. He suddenly became conscious of his outburst.

It was after a very long silence that he spoke out, as if in explanation, 'Tania and I are getting a divorce.'

The two of them sat drinking late into the night. Raghu's meeting the next day was destined to be a routine one.

A river runs through it

When Raghu woke up with his hangover the next morning, Nandini was all packed and about to leave. She was going away to visit her parents in Allahabad. This was a trip which Raghu ordinarily much looked forward to. It was his biannual quota of rationed bachelorhood and he held it just short of sacred. Today, however, was different. Today it was not respite but a sense of impending emptiness that seemed to loom ominously over him.

Barely had he stirred in bed when Nandini started off with her last-moment instructions on domestic imperatives. He somehow managed to open his eyes to a seemingly sufficient degree. Then in the middle of it all, he abruptly mumbled, 'Don't go.' She was taken aback. Her instinct could immediately sense that this 'don't go' was different. It wasn't the near carnal 'don't go' from the first three months of their marriage. It wasn't the farcical 'don't go' of the very next year. And it wasn't the rotting 'don't go' of the year after that—the 'don't go' which eventually had to be retired.

It would be futile to go into the details of what followed. And futile also to judge the Kumars for allowing Nandini's trip to go on as scheduled. In a prosaic world of sanctioned leaves and non-refundable airline tickets, such an outcome was all but inevitable.

Raghu ambled about the house aimlessly and after having tried a couple of the usual distractions, finally settled for the most passive of them all—television. But even the mesmerizing glow of the devil's eye couldn't keep him amused for long. He was battling a restless emptiness, not boredom. The fact was that Abhay's outburst had shaken him up. And though he would have liked to believe (indeed, *would* believe, when recollecting the incident a couple of years from now) that it was concern for Abhay which had kept him awake till the wee hours of the morning, the truth was different. Yes, there had been concern, and a very sincere one at that, but what towered above that concern was personal anguish coupled with a sense of vacuity.

Raghu had looked up to Abhay almost all his life. It was an admiration which had over the years been stripped quite clean of even that faithful adherent—envy (so disparate were their respective achievements that the reach of his envy usually fell well short of Abhay. And so robust was their longstanding bond that Raghu had subconsciously started to regard Abhay's achievements as his own.) Therefore, what in school had begun as simple awe-inspired emulation had by youth atrophied into a sort of moral indolence. Abhay's opinion—not only that which Raghu sought, but also the one which he imagined ('What would Abhay have done/said in this situation?') became the touchstone of his decisions. Whether it was day-to-day ethics or long-term goals, Raghu could rarely bring himself to think beyond the examples set by Abhay.

This gradual debilitation of ability to decipher one's own mind, along with a tendency to be swayed by the opinion of others, is a fairly common affliction. But what made it different in Raghu's case was that it had been wrought upon him by a single individual, and not by societal trends. The risks, therefore, weren't spread out. All bets were centered on a single idol. And now that warring idol had suddenly dropped his weapons and turned away from battle—that too a battle he had been on top of. Hell! If pots of money, a gleaming societal reputation, and a beautiful and doting wife did not hold the answers to a happy life, Raghu was damned if he knew what did.

Courage, it is said, wasn't the only quality that Alexander's generals acquired from him. Legend has it that most of them even walked like him—with the head tilted to one side.

Indeed, great can be the slant that idols create.

The week went by uneventfully. A conceited fear that he would galvanise Abhay's decision to sell off kept Raghu from calling up Abhay. Then as the weekend set in and the disquiet mounted, he packed his bag and took off to Niranjanpur.

Niranjanpur was a sleepy small town in the hills of Himachal where Abeer had been living for the past ten years.

Abeer, after his engineering, had taken the civil services exam and had gone on to become an IAS officer. He had thought it to be the most expedient way of doing something meaningful for others. When asked about his choice of career during the training program in Mussoorie, he had in a moment of unguarded youthful fervor remarked, 'If I do well in my job, I could make a difference in the lives of a million.'

It took three years for that conviction to shatter. But characteristically, his was not the type of disillusionment that was preceded by bouts of heated arguments and episodes of rubbing influential people the wrong way. Ground realities revealed themselves to him somewhat more gently. Each passing week at work made it gradually clear to the observant Abeer that the powers vested in him were scarcely commensurate with the kind of ends he had in mind. Finally, on a fine Monday morning, after he had at leisure contemplated the ramifications of his decision, he tendered his resignation.

He had walked out of the secretariat devoid of any bitterness or ill feeling. Then after spending a week with his parents, and another with Abhay and Raghu, he finally came over to live in Niranjanpur, the town of his ancestors.

On the banks of the river Tripti, Niranjanpur was a town possessed of a beauty at once subdued and furtive. One fell in love with the town not at first glance but gradually; and hence, more enduringly.

As for Abeer's family home, it was an old and majestic structure situated by the riverside. Everyone in Niranjanpur referred to it as the *haveli*. Like most idyllic edifices which go by that name, this one too was in dire need of repair. Abeer had wasted absolutely no time in setting about that task. His modest inheritance from the maternal side—coupled with his meager savings and a loan from his dad—had been pumped into phase one of project resurrection; and within four months of his arrival, fifteen odd rooms had been brought around to a safe and habitable condition.

Abeer started his residential school in those fifteen rooms. The ensuing years proved to be benignly eventful and saw the school make progress in both scale and reputation. Today, the *haveli* stood entirely renovated.

⚘

Eight years had passed since Raghu and Abeer had last met. Considering what they had once meant to each other, Raghu couldn't help wondering how things had come to such a pass.

They had obviously kept in regular touch for the first few years after college. Then distance gradually began to get the better of them. Mails and telephone calls got sparser with passing time till they were reduced to the mandatory ones on birthdays, anniversaries, and big holidays. No one was to blame actually, for there is only so much that a telephone call or mail is capable of. The best conversations that happen between friends are usually the ones that grow out of languid silences. And there is no such thing as a silent mail or phone call. Of course, there is also the issue of mismatched moods and circumstances. One single perky and frivolous phone call that is answered back in a business-like tone (no matter how genuinely engaged the person adopting that tone may be) serves to instate a month-long moratorium on future endeavors of its kind. Two such consecutive incidents and the moratorium could run up to half a year. Three, and the fate of frivolity is sealed. What remain are the birthdays and anniversaries.

Raghu, half reclined on the back seat of his taxi, couldn't help hypothesizing how Abeer would have changed in this while. There was the initial temptation of giving in to the romantic '... no matter after how long we meet, we always pick the threads of our friendship from where we'd left them last', but Raghu was too much of a pragmatist to believe in that. He well knew that two people separated by time and distance were likely to ripen in their own different ways. During their separation, the atoms of experience which each gathered were bound to be different, and hence the personalities which these atoms in turn moulded were bound to be different. Also, assuming that one of them hadn't in fact changed, it was obvious that he would *appear* different to the altered perceptions of the other. So one way or another, it was back to the wall! No, concluded Raghu, the thread theory was absolutely no good. That theory was at best a temporary illusion; one that could sustain as long as those laboring under it confined themselves to the common ground of past acquaintances and experience ('How's so and so? Do you remember the time when...')

The actual meeting turned out to be quite a mixed bag. First impressions indicated that Abeer was much the same; his welcome was warm yet unostentatious, he looked as unassuming as always, and he still blurted things with characteristic plainness of manner. In short, he was still very simple.

Yet, despite all that genuine warmth, it somehow didn't seem like old times. A wall appeared to have cropped up between them. It was a faint and frail wall, but it was nonetheless a structure that impeded free passage. Even as Raghu hurled those seemingly inadvertent genial abuses at Abeer (that puerile acid test which friendship is so often subjected to) he became more aware of that barrier. Time alone was to tell whether it was a permanent fixture or one that would wear away with renewed acquaintance.

The threads, though found and picked up, hadn't quite been untangled.

'Do you still play?' asked Raghu as they walked past a soccer ground. The question had come out almost in reflex—a subconscious effort to steer the conversation towards a common and comfortable past.

'Almost every day,' replied Abeer. Then perceiving his response as too reticent, he went on to make some references to their Scad days.

It was evening time and Abeer was showing Raghu around the school. They had been indulging in that small talk which is the necessary bane of friends meeting after long. And though some short silences had started to thrive, the longer ones—those that are a true measure of compatibility—still gasped with discomfort. The wall didn't look to give away so easily.

They had walked up to the end of the corridor and could either turn back or move on to the next floor. It took but a few moments of eye to eye conferring to decide. They opted for the stairs, which, being steep and arduous to negotiate, served as good camouflage for another much needed interlude of quiet. But like the other interludes that had preceded it, this one too ripened rapidly and was presently on the verge of putrefying. Raghu plucked it off with a Scad motif. 'Your experience of a boarding school—did it help in designing the curriculum here?'

'Uh...yes it did,' answered Abeer with just the slightest bit of hesitation. It was evident that he wanted to say more. Raghu recognized the hesitation for what it was—a polite concern for the listener—and gestured Abeer to go on.

'You remember my quitting the civil services,' began Abeer.

'Don't tell me we're deriving this from first principles!' retorted Raghu. Abeer smiled. The first assault at the wall was an inadvertent one and it had come off well.

'You were very angry at my decision,' went on Abeer. 'Perhaps because I'd given rather vague reasons for it,' he added, as if to justify on Raghu's behalf.

'You had said it was none of my business,' interjected Raghu. The bitterness was unadorned. 'The same words,' he went on reflexively, for this was an issue he had mulled over many times in solitude, 'from anyone else—even Abhay—wouldn't have hurt so much.'

Abeer was touched by the preference shown to him, even though he knew that the real reason behind it wasn't the one which Raghu imagined. Each individual friendship is built on an exclusive foundation. And because each foundation is exclusive, every friendship has exclusive nuances to its code of conduct; thereby allowing one single action to hold different implications for different friendships of equal standing. The same action, hence, could in one case be considered acceptable, and in the other be called a breach of code.

Abeer wished he could explain to Raghu that it was a simple breach of code, and not something deeply sinister, which had caused the two-year hiatus in their relationship. But he chose not to say that. He recalled that they had first resumed talking only on the occasion of Vini's birth, and that though they had been in touch ever since, both had taken care not to meander anywhere near the frayed nerves. Abeer allowed that prudence to prevail. He opted in favour of a clarification.

'I wasn't ready to share my notions with anybody,' he explained. 'They seemed too far-fetched and absurd, even by my standards.' The 'even by my standards' was his feeble attempt at humor—a little something to hedge the risks of the topic he was broaching.

'Far-fetched? This school? C'mon, thousands of schools pop up in the country each year. What's far-fetched about starting a school?'

'I guess that brings us to your first question; about my

experience in Scad being of use here,' replied Abeer. 'Because wanting to start a school may not be far-fetched, but wanting to deviate from a successful model like Scad definitely is.'

They had walked up to a spot from where the river was fully visible. A deep sigh escaped Raghu, quite in keeping with the view's reputation of being a breathtaking one. He stood congealed and spellbound, and time lingered on and the silence didn't once beg to be broken. When he finally spoke, it wasn't to make small talk.

'It couldn't have been that bad.'

Abeer, realizing that the allusion was to his civil services job, answered 'No it wasn't.'

'Then why'd you quit?'

'A couple of reasons actually...but mainly because of a fascinating phenomenon. I was quite taken by it and was keen to implement it.'

'And hence the school?'

'And hence the school.'

'And what, if I may ask, was the phenomenon?'

Abeer took some time before he answered 'The slow and systematic transformation of my batchmates. I say systematic because it couldn't have been otherwise.'

'And what you mean by transformation is a shedding of wings and the growing of a pair of horns along with a tail.' The little outburst a few minutes ago had left Raghu with two choices. He could either put on a solemn air for the rest of the evening, or he could break the ice with a bit of pertness. For practical reasons he had chosen the latter.

'Nothing that drastic,' laughed Abeer. 'But yes, if you're going to define proclivities in terms of wings and horns, ours was very much an average batch. We had the standard 15-70-

15 distribution of a normal bell curve. And mind you, these fault lines were pretty distinct. They were evident for all to see even before the end of the year-long stay in the academy.' He waited a while before he started to elaborate. 'The first fifteen per cent were pretty clear about the money and power they were there for. They were almost unapologetic about it too, and consequently, willing to do what it took. Those who played their cards right, flourished.'

'Let me guess. The fifteen percent at the other end were those with the *keeda*,' declared Raghu.

'Not exactly. You couldn't call those guys naïvely patriotic, but yes, they definitely wanted to do something for the society and country—wanted to bring about a positive change in the so-called system.'

'*Watan pe jo fida hoga, bahut hi chu...*'

'The change-seekers further branched out into two groups,' cut in Abeer, not quite willing to let Raghu finish his juvenile rhyme. 'The first was the "honest" set—guys who were ramrod straight and who held the written rule to be sacrosanct; they never gave a damn about whom they were pitted against in their battle to uphold it. Predictably, they were eventually consigned to meaningless postings—"*thanda bastaas*" as we call them. The second set comprised of those who made certain concessions with their honesty but kept their integrity intact. These were people who were concerned not with battles but with the war. They knew that the first prerequisite to changing the system was being in a position that allowed them to do so.

'Mind you, it's due to no small contribution from these select few that the fabled steel frame of Indian democracy is able to hold.'

'And all of *this* is what you found to be fascinating,' mocked

Raghu in a bored sounding tone. The chinks in the wall were beginning to show. Abeer, who was pleased to see them too, smiled when he answered, 'Yes, quite. But what *really* fascinated me, what in effect prompted me to start this school...' Raghu looked at him with a start as Abeer revealed, 'was the remaining seventy percent. The fence sitters—guys who could have gone either way but who slowly but surely, in varying extents, fell into the mould of the first fifteen.'

'What were they to do? Bask in the ridicule of their peers, staff, and political masters? Hell, even their own family! But please tell me that we haven't got to the fascinating part yet.'.

'The fascinating part is that not only in the services but in all walks of life, the majority of people are fence sitters; people who could sway in either direction because they're inordinately vulnerable to the influences that surround them. Also, it's important to note that fence sitting has no correlation with intelligence. A genius could be a fence sitter.'

It was with a mischievous smile that Raghu asked, 'And your school trains these fence sitters to go the right way.'

'Not exactly,' replied Abeer. 'The school enables them to *choose* their own way. As I just said, it's not as if fence sitters are low on intelligence or acumen. It's just that their opinion forming muscle was left weak from lack of exercise. The lack could be because an overbearing parent obviated the need of decision taking, or it could be because too many occasions for decision taking didn't actually arise. There could well be a hundred reasons.

'The crux is that a majority of people never take the trouble of thinking for themselves. Consequently, they're very susceptible and pliable to the opinions that bombard them.'

'But isn't pliable what we're encouraged to be? I mean, what with that example about mighty trees being uprooted in the face of a strong wind, and the flexible reed bending over and holding its own. I thought it was a virtue being pliable.'

'It *is* a virtue,' agreed Abeer, 'but only when it's done voluntarily. It is no virtue when you lose the faculty of thinking for yourself, and your peers and surroundings start to shape all your tastes, desires and convictions. In fact, so dependent are some people on the opinion of others that even their happiness is incomplete until it has been acknowledged by others.'

Raghu felt the uncomfortable tug of an ailment recently diagnosed.

'Take our Scad days for example,' went on Abeer, 'Specifically, Scad dinner time. Do you remember how sought after *paneer* was?'

Raghu nodded. 'We were allowed just a fixed number of pieces.'

'Right,' said Abeer, 'and if you didn't want your share, you *bequeathed* it to someone else. Well I didn't like *paneer* and would always pass it up. Then one day, prompted by the clamor that my allotted five pieces caused among the tablemates, I decided to give paneer a go and...'

'And you didn't find it so bad. Then over time, you actually started to relish it,' finished Raghu.

'Yes. And so is the way with most of our aspirations. They're picked up inadvertently, much in the manner we pick up contagious germs.'

'But there *is* such a thing called acquired taste,' Raghu objected, 'I mean, I didn't take to classical music immediately. It took me a while to learn and appreciate it.'

'Wonderful point! Because it leads us to infer that contagious germs aren't always malignant. They can be benign too.'

'And how do you decide?' demanded Raghu. 'Ambition, for example. If someone inspires you to be ambitious, is that a benign influence or a malignant one?' He had somehow managed to say that in a manner which made it seem that his interest in the subject was purely academic.

'The answer to your first question—I don't decide. And nor do I think that anyone else should. At the school too, the effort isn't to push the boys down a trail. The effort is to make them capable of choosing their own path—one that's in accordance with their intrinsic nature.'

'C'mon! Kids and intrinsic nature! Aren't they a bit too young for that?'

'On the contrary,' replied Abeer 'The younger they are, the more free they're likely to be and closer to their intrinsic nature. Because call it Chomsky and Fodor's genetically transmitted "innate knowledge"—something like language—or call it Vedanta's accumulated *samskaras*; there *is* such a thing as intrinsic nature. And one way to get in touch with it is to break down all experience into a two-step process. Step one—be consciously aware of all opinions and influences you are bombarded with. Step two—filter those influences through your intrinsic nature before you assign them a status.'

'But intrinsic nature *is* what we're trying to find out,' objected Raghu.

'Need I remind you how higher-degree polynomial equations are solved? You begin with approximations. Then after reviewing the results obtained by using those approximations, you work your way closer to the solution. Here too, step one assists in step two, and step two makes for a better step one. As you start to analyze the influences upon you, you tend to know more about yourself. And as you get to know more about yourself, you are able to better analyze the subsequent influences. It's an ongoing phenomenon and you keep getting better at it.

'You mentioned ambition. Let's run it through the two steps. Step one requires that you fully analyze this invading emotion. What vehicle has it come riding on? (Is it jealousy of a peer? Is it inspiration from a superior? Or is it a gnawing vacuum from within?) What language is it speaking? (Is it the tongue of material possessions? Or is it the dialect of climbing up the social ladder?) Etcetera, etcetera.

'Now step two tries to determine what the said ambition *really* means to you. Needless to say, it uses answers from step one to put things into perspective.'

'Doesn't sound easy, that second step.'

'Not easy at all. Which is why we make use of tools. In the case of ambition, for example, you could use a tool such as the thirty-three per cent test.'

'Go on!'

'Let's assume that you aspire to own a seven series BMW. Or let's say that you wish to take an adventure trip to the South Pole. Now let's also assume that after much toil you're able to put together the resources for the said dream. Then just as you're about to sign on the dotted line, along comes this person to sweeten the deal for you. He offers you a discount of thirty-three per cent. The only catch, he says, is that none of your acquaintances are to ever know of your car; or your trip, as the case may be. So much so that you're not even allowed to post pictures on social networks. Now, the question is, would you go ahead with the deal at the discount? Or would the constraints urge you to demand a larger reduction?

'Well if you find the thirty-three per cent concession attractive, you're one of those rare people who appreciate the art in machinery, or have a genuine love for travel. But if your desired discount—the discount below which you'll not accept the constraints—is in the vicinity of fifty per cent and above...'

'...as it most likely would be in the belt where I live... laughed Raghu.

Abeer allowed himself only a very faint smile. Mocking did not come easily to him. 'My advice to such people would be that they reassess their wants; that they seek out new aspirations where the desired discount isn't so high.

'So you see, it's not as if we've bluntly shattered material aspirations with a sledge hammer. All we've done is chipped away at the spurious part of their appeal. As time goes by and all spurious scales fall away, what's left is the true core—a core, mind you, that varies from person to person. Which is why everyone needs to ferret out *their* own core.'

'So happiness,' surmised Raghu 'doesn't come in a common standard packing. According to you it is different things to different people.'

'Quite,' affirmed Abeer.

'All right,' said Raghu after some thought, 'I get the drift about our environment and peers shaping our desires. But tell me, what's so wrong about showing off my BMW or my expedition memoirs? I mean, if my chief thrill in life lies in seeking admiration and acclaim from people, and provided that I am successful in obtaining it, then what is it that could screw my trip? Agreed, it would be a life which the wise call shallow, but to hell with the wise and their sour grapes. The question is...what...could... screw...my...trip? What is it that would prevent me from being happy at a practical level?'

'I guess that one of the two things would happen at the practical level. You would either run out of things to show off, or you would run out of people to show them to. Because come to think of it, you can show off one achievement to one set of people only once. Besides, there is also the question of finding an eligible audience. No point in impressing people whose opinion doesn't matter to you.'

Raghu lit up a cigarette and puffed at it languorously. He watched the smoke as it dissipated.

'It doesn't take long for an aware person,' continued Abeer, 'to spot the paradox that's public adulation. Surprising isn't it, that one pays heed to the *collective mass* and yet has no great respect for any of the *individuals* that comprise it? So you see, it's just a matter of time before an aware man weans away from the craving for public adulation. He moves on to praise from a select few—those whom he has regard for. Mind you, he *needs* this praise. He needs it because no matter how confident he might look, he is still not so sure of himself on a lot of issues. There is still time for that.'

Raghu was suddenly reminded of a slightly risqué remark that he had made at a social gathering. The impropriety of the remark's wording had kept him tossing and turning till late in the night. And yet, when he received a couple of approving phone calls the next morning, that same wording had seemed genuinely witty to him.

'And till that time arrives,' said Abeer, 'the young minds need to be given more and more practice with steps one and two. When an idea is hurled at them, they should be able to break it down into its constituting elements of fact, rhetoric and conjecture. They should be able to judge which emotion that idea plays upon; which prejudice it incites. And though they should acknowledge the reputation of the idea's source, they should not be swayed by it blindly. They should be aware that a man reputed for wisdom is not immune from the occasional idiocy, and that a fool might yet be capable of offering a valuable lesson. In a nutshell, they should be able to strip away the irrational component of influence that accompanies all stimuli. Because if they fail to do so, all their learning would be quite useless..'

'Aren't we going a bit overboard?' put in Raghu, this time without the affected sarcasm.

Abeer's reply was immediate, as if he had preempted the question. 'Ask any doctor about his diagnosis gaffes during OPD training when upon even a slight correlation of symptoms, his patient appeared to be suffering with that very same disease which he had studied the previous night. I think they call it the MBBS syndrome.'

Raghu let out a little laugh.

'It would be no laughing matter,' continued Abeer, 'if the doctors were to not outgrow that vulnerability to influence. And yet we think nothing of the way in which names, numbers, reputations, and even sheer volubility are able to influence us.'

Raghu started to say something but checked himself midway.

'Read up any renowned philosopher,' went on Abeer 'and you'll find yourself nodding in agreement to a lot of things. Then read up another eminent one a couple of weeks later and you'll find yourself nodding to him too, without once realizing that the two belong to absolutely different schools of thought. The thing that made you nod was the overpowering influence of their reputations. It's like walking straight into the Montaigne trap. Montaigne,' elaborated Abeer, 'compares the unsuccessful seeker to a man who goes looking for fire for his hearth; but when he gets to bask in the warmth of a neighbour's already lit fireside, he forgets all about the light which he was to carry back home.'

'And what does Montaigne compare the successful seeker

to?' the smirk was back.

'To the honeybee—which collects nectar from different flowers, and then works on it to convert it into something even sweeter.'

Raghu had asked the question as a playful teaser, but the pertinence of the allegory didn't fail to get to him. 'And then there's the convenience of bottled honey,' he mumbled.

It had gotten dark and Abeer suggested that they proceed for dinner. As they ambled towards the students' mess, he casually told Raghu about how they had retained the Scad system of having a fixed menu for each day of the week. 'Today being a Saturday,' he went on to inform, 'we may well look forward to some *paneer*.'

The apprentices

> *Through not observing what is in the mind of another, a man has seldom been seen to be unhappy; but those who do not observe the movements of their own minds must of necessity be unhappy.*
> —Marcus Aurelius

The lines were written on a board in the assembly hall, and to Raghu they seemed like a good buttress to the discussion he had the previous evening. Raghu tried to read the contents of the next board but couldn't. The proceedings of the morning assembly had started.

Abeer walked in, wished everyone a good morning, said the prayers, and read out a number from a pad on his lectern. The piano started to play and soon everyone joined in to sing the prayer song. Raghu smiled. It was all too reminiscent of Scad. The number which Abeer had randomly picked out was a code for the song that was being sung. Today, irrespective of their professed religion, 500-odd boys were beckoning Allah at the top of their voices to save them from vice. It was Iqbal's *Lub pe aati hai dua banke* that rented the air.

The song was followed by a welcome note extended to Raghu on behalf of the school, trailing which came announcements relevant to the boys' day-to-day schedule. This faithful lifting of the Scad assembly routine obviously tickled the imp in Raghu. Quips—with which he intended to badger Abeer—began to take nebulous shape. But even before he could polish any of them with a deft touch or two, he heard the words 'News please' being called out. On cue, a boy aged about sixteen walked up to the dais and started to read out the news. Raghu found it surprising that the headlines were those from the previous day. But then something even more surprising happened. The boy started to elaborate upon each headline and went on to explain its relevance and implication. It was obvious that these were *his* interpretations. It was obvious because the conjectures that had been employed were typical of his age. Once the boy had finished, Abeer made a few suggestions to fill out some obvious holes in the boy's logic. He then patted the boy on his back and assembly was over.

'What was all that?' asked Raghu as they sat sipping coffee in Abeer's office.

'News,' answered Abeer, 'Though a few of my boys—the ones averse to public speaking—call it noose.'

'I don't blame them, hangman,' grinned Raghu as he added, 'One of your form-your-own-opinion exercises?'

Abeer smiled in agreement.

'And everyone has to do it?'

'Ninth grade onwards, yes.'

'It must be a dreadful experience for most guys—making a fool of themselves before the whole school.'

'Not as dreadful as you think. I mean, since it is done every day, and everyone has to do it at some point of time, there's very little sense of "occasion" to the whole thing. They soon acclimatize to it.'

Abeer discharged a waiting peon with some brief instructions before he continued, 'Your other concern—about the boys making a fool of themselves—is slightly more valid. But that too is quelled by a corollary of the previous argument. You see, since nobody wants to be branded a fool before the whole school, they learn to get good at the game. They start to learn even before they get to class nine and, propelled by habit, keep learning even once their turn is over.'

'But how do they, as you call it, *learn*?'

'Quite in the manner that you saw today—the boy makes his analysis and I fill in the gaps where necessary. Also, since the operation is carried out in full view, every student gets fully acquainted with the tools that are used to dissect events and opinions. And once acquainted, it's just a matter of time before they start to use those tools by themselves. Eventually, they learn to use them well; and they learn to use them on things other than news.'

It wasn't long before an impish smile made its way to Raghu's lips. 'And what makes you so sure that the boys don't cheat? After all, it was day-old news that the boy was analyzing. He had time on his hands. What stopped him from seeking help?'

'The school's culture,' was the matter-of-fact reply.

'Ah! The school's culture,' said Raghu with a drawn out drawl dipped in sarcasm. The wall had all but crumbled. 'But seriously, do you import all your students from some sort of utopia? Because I know that I went to some of the best institutions in the country and *they* couldn't keep me from cheating. I mean, I don't need to remind you that I *did* copy some of my assignments. That's culture for you.'

Abeer took his time to rally his answer into coherence. 'Culture,' he started, 'like conscience, is just another name that we give to the habits of a society. And habits can change because...'

'Just...just a minute,' butted in Raghu. 'Now conscience definitely is more than a societal habit.'

'Is it? Then why doesn't the conscience of a man from a feudal village prick him when he hits his wife, whereas that of an elite Mumbai banker does? Anyway, that's not what we were discussing.'

'You were telling me how habits change. So go on. Tell me how they changed in *your* school.'

'Well it helped that we started out small. The boys and I got to know each other well. So when I told them that I will not tolerate lies, and followed that up in deed and example, they kind of followed suit. When anyone reneged, I'd simply skip my next three meals and restrict my communication with them to a bare minimum.'

'And that stopped the lying?' asked Raghu with surprise.

Abeer smiled in affirmation.

'Well only because you're an affable bastard,' accused Raghu.

'Or because the mess staff took advantage of my absence and served them bland stuff in that while,' laughed Abeer. 'The interesting thing is that I didn't have to skip meals even when new boys joined. As if automatically, they got dyed in the school culture that had come to prevail.'

Raghu was reminded of some of his previous workplaces. The ones with a culture of sincerity had indeed not allowed shirkers and idlers to thrive. And vice versa. In both cases, the oddballs had either been reformed or were flushed out.

'How about a walk?' proposed Abeer, breaking Raghu's short trance.

They walked down the corridors and the conversation sauntered around the boys and the school. Abeer explained how—despite the various changes he had effected—the school in its day to day endeavors retained coherence with other educational institutions. There was emphasis on sports and physical well being. And the students were encouraged to do well in the prescribed academic formats.

He then went on to inform about the challenges which faced him; prime among them being getting good teachers on board. Abeer felt that since kids imbibed most of their values through observation, and rarely from instruction, the responsibility of a teacher as role model couldn't be stressed enough. More so in a residential school where a teacher's demeanor was open for round-the-clock scrutiny.

'In Finland,' spoke Abeer, 'they allow only their brightest and most passionate to pursue the career of a teacher. Befitting, I would say. When you intend someone to shape your kid's character and draw out her talents, you'd want that person to be the very best. So it's only obvious that Finnish teachers are both highly paid and highly respected. And when I say respect I mean genuine respect; not empty lip-service that's given to "Master sahabs" and "sirs".'

'So how did Master Abeer Bajwa manage to recruit others of his ilk?'

Abeer explained how his starting out small had, once again, turned out to be a blessing in disguise. He recalled how his first recruitment had featured a vacancy for just three teachers. And the three which he picked were—by a stroke of luck—fairly above average in aptitude and dedication. Then eventually, with a mentoring that was abetted by close proximity, all three blossomed into something quite exceptional. It did of course help that they were handsomely paid. 'The money came by opting away from some needless ostentation.'

The second bout of recruitment was more difficult. Though there was no dearth of applications, the right candidates just didn't seem to be coming through. Weeks went by. Four people continued to do the work of six but did not once yield to the temptation of lowering the benchmark. So when they *did* ultimately secure their candidates, they had also secured alongside a noteworthy reputation for themselves. The school came to be known for a staff that was both elite and very well paid. People in the teaching profession wanted to break into those ranks simply because it was difficult to do so.

'Quite an effort you're putting in here,' remarked Raghu after some thought, 'but honestly, I still don't get the big picture.'

'What big picture?'

'Well you left the services for *this*. Surely you have something up your sleeve. Perhaps some sort of a revolution that you're gearing up for.'

Abeer laughed aloud. 'You flatter me, Kumar! Tell me, what revolution could possibly brew in a laidback small-town school?'

Raghu didn't attempt any wisecrack and Abeer continued.

'Besides, I'm not much of a believer in revolutions. In the old Rousseau-Voltaire spectrum, my position would be about three quarters towards the Voltaire end. History is too replete with examples of failed revolutions.'

'Is it?' objected Raghu, apparently armed with examples that supported his challenge.

Abeer preempted the argument. 'Agreed, many a revolution was successful in its first objective—overthrowing the existing system. But tell me, how many of them got around to replacing the old system with something substantially better?'

No answer came to Raghu's mind.

'Anyway,' went on Abeer, 'even if revolutions were a successful mode of reform, I think they would hardly be suited to a mild personality like mine. So I guess I'll leave the induction of drastic change to better men. Let *them* usher in the new world. In the meanwhile, I'll just help a bunch of kids find happiness in the present one.'

'A wise move too,' said Raghu, 'because I don't see any of those drastic changes happening anytime soon. Vice—for lack of a less corny word—is a blue chip share. Its price may take the occasional beating but in the long run, we can absolutely bank on it.'

A couple of boys wished Abeer and Raghu as they walked past them. So pleasant was their manner that Raghu halted, turned, and kept looking at them till they had walked away around the corner. 'Tell me,' he implored Abeer, with his eyes still fixed at the vacant corner, 'aren't you really creating misfits here? I mean, they don't lie, they don't cheat, and they smile like morons, as if they're actually happy or something.'

Abeer let out a hearty laugh. 'But that's where our definitions of misfit vary. For you a misfit is somebody who hasn't adapted to the ways of society, and his best bet to happiness lies in his doing so. Whereas for me, a misfit is one who isn't happy. For him, the best bet to happiness lies in his being at peace with society, and not necessarily in adapting to its ways.'

'Isn't that absurd? To not adapt to society's ways and yet be at peace with it.'

'Not at all!' asserted Abeer. 'On the contrary, it's absurd to not adapt to society's ways and yet not be at peace with it.'

'If it doesn't sound crazy, it's not Abeer,' said Raghu with a shake of his head.

'It's true,' protested Abeer, 'But to get a better grasp of it, you'd need to dissect "not adapting to society's ways."

'When we say that someone, say X, is not adapting to society's ways, what we're broadly referring to are the two main differences between X and *society*. The differences of *do*s and *don't*s. The differences in *do*s are the different goals which each pursue. And the differences in *don't*s are the different things which each proclaim to shun—let's call them vices, for lack of a less corny word.' Raghu smarted at the playful ribbing of 'corny' but allowed it to pass, and Abeer continued, 'Now the interesting part is that it's X, and not society, who is responsible for all the trouble that's born out of these differences.'

'Is it?'

'Think about it. Look at the first difference for example. I mean, why should society have a problem if X's goals are different than its own? Because not only does that difference reduce competition, it also ensures that society needn't feel jealous of the goals which X has achieved. Those goals are meaningless to it.

'So if there's any problem with the first difference, it's mainly in X's mind. It's him who—in the face of a strong contra influence—needs to hold on to the belief that his goal is worthwhile. And more often than not, holding on to that belief is the major source of X's anxiety.'

'But how's X to blame when the vices are different?' asked Raghu.

'In a lot of ways actually. But mainly because of his self righteousness. When X conquers a vice—especially such a one that society finds difficult to overcome—an air of self righteousness invariably crops up alongside. It is an air which is noxious to all those who haven't made that conquest. And hence the trouble between X and society.'

'Surely, not everyone who's above a vice wears such an air.'

'Well depending upon taste and upbringing, people may choose to wear that air covertly, obliquely or explicitly. But wear it they do. C'mon, when people can be proud of their idiosyncrasies—even the absolutely inconsequential ones—they can obviously be proud of their attainments.' Abeer assumed two different tones so as to impersonate two different characters. 'I haven't had a cup of tea in the last twenty years,' he mimicked in the first voice, and then using the second, added, 'I can't get out of bed till I've had my cup of tea.'

Raghu smiled.

'But it's true! Anyway, my point is that if people are so pompous about a cup of tea, you can imagine how swollen-up they're bound to be about something which they've worked to achieve.'

'What you're saying is that self righteousness will *always* accompany the overcoming of vice.'

'Unless of course one works to prevent it. For example, let's say you have to cut down on your calorie intake and move towards a healthier diet. The first…'

'Cut out the parallels,' interjected Raghu. 'If you're going to use examples, use ones with real vice.'

'But gluttony *is* a vice,' smiled Abeer and proceeded 'So, as I was saying, there could be two ways to move to a healthier low-calorie diet. One way of doing it could be through sheer self control and willpower. It's the most common way. The second way could be that of reason—the way where a person methodically and diligently weighs his options. And when he finally picks the healthy diet, he does so because he clearly perceives its inherent advantages.'

'But in the end,' objected Raghu, 'the person who takes to the diet out of willpower also reaps the same benefits. Besides, there's an involvement of will power in the second case too. So where's the difference?'

'The difference lies in the quality of knowledge. To the person in the first case, the link between a healthy diet and a healthy body is diaphanous and hazy. Not that he doesn't believe in the link, just that its relevance is greatly diminished. It's diminished because he finds the road between cause and effect to be a long and circuitous one. Conversely, for the second chap, the link is clear and present. He *knows* the benefits of a healthy diet. He's *aware* of its repercussions on his body weight, blood pressure, and cholesterol. And because he knows, he doesn't miss out on sensing the enhanced energy levels which the diet begets. Nor does he underestimate the glorious feeling of a full bowel movement every morning. Therefore, when he compares all these advantages with the competing advantage—advantage, I repeat, not sin—of taste pleasures, he finds the scales tilted in favour of the former. So ultimately, not too much of will power gets involved when he takes to that balanced healthy diet.'

'Still, the only difference between your two vice-conquering guys lies in their methods of reaching their goals. The important question is, is it any different *after* that?'

'After that, the difference lies in a hot chocolate fudge.'

'Come again!'

'It lies in how each of them views a third person enjoying a hot chocolate fudge.'

'Ah! You mean the presence and absence of self righteousness,' remarked Raghu, a tad sarcastically.

'Precisely. Because self righteousness, where present, will distill resentment from deprivation. Then after mixing that resentment with generous doses of synthetic sanctimoniousness, it will complete the noxious cocktail by sprinkling a dash of envy which though poorly disguised, will nevertheless insist on lying to you about its real name.'

'Some poetic bar-keeping that!'

Abeer made a mock bow of acknowledgement and continued 'Contrarily, our man of reason is spared these emotions. In fact, should the person having the chocolate fudge be an overweight one, the emotions incited in our man are those of concern and compassion. So you see, not only is there less strain on our man to give in to temptation, he's also more at peace with society.'

'But c'mon, you can't have purely logical reasons against all vices.'

'Yes you can. Okay, some of them won't be as cogent as others, but that really doesn't matter. Because eventually, one attains to a demeanor that transcends even reason. After sticking to a healthy wholesome diet for years together, the fried stuff simply ceases to appeal.'

Raghu waited before he spoke, as if summing things up for himself. 'So in a nutshell, what we have here is a bunch of guys striving towards certain objectives. And though these objectives are by and large common to all, they have been customized by each person according to his own distinct personality. Importantly, this striving is done not out of concern for heaven or hell, but because of a belief that the objectives *by themselves* would lead to enduring happiness. And finally, the tools employed to achieve the objectives are tools of reason, not of willpower.'

'Coudn't have put it better myself,' smiled Abeer

'And yet,' smiled back Raghu, a smile that was clearly pregnant with the clincher, 'and yet you used emotional blackmail to make the boys give up lying.'

'Hardly,' answered Monket with calm, 'I didn't talk to them because in that very act lay a message.'

'Message?'

'The message that lying renders all communication useless.'

After a pause Abeer continued, 'But since you're so keen to poke a hole in the arrangement here, let me apprise you with a paradox. You see, though we aim to develop individuality, we nevertheless seek assistance from the safety of numbers. We want boys to think for themselves, but our main aid in achieving that end is the example of other boys who're already doing so.'

'Might as well tell me your excuse for doing it.'

Abeer laughed. Their long-standing bond had just become apparent in Raghu's prescience.

'The excuse is actually a long and true story. But let me cut it short for you.'

'Please!'

'The story's about this guy living in America who's diagnosed with cancer. Doctors give him nine months to live and he decides to spend them on his native Greek island of Ikaria. As you might have guessed, he doesn't die after those allotted nine months. He in fact outlives the very doctors who'd predicted his death. This story gets around and some journalists take notice that it's in fact common for most Ikarians to live to their nineties. Researchers find this interesting. They start to look for reasons behind the miracle. They cite the Mediterranean diet, the healthy ocean air, the pollution-free surroundings, the laidback and stress-free atmosphere, even genetics. But the explanation doesn't entirely fit; because the nearby islands also possess most of these features while the life expectancy there isn't so high.

'Then one small difference emerges. Whereas the atmosphere in other islands is *conducive* to a stress-free life, it is only in Ikaria that such a life is actually lived. Indeed, the majority of Ikarians are a laid-back lot. And in their being laid-back lies a part of the secret to their longevity. But just a small part, mind you! The major part—the crucial part of the secret—lies elsewhere. It's that part which is the main take-away of our story.'

'And that is?' asked Raghu, somewhat impatiently.

'That it's far easier to be laidback and stress-free when everyone around you is that way. It's true! Most of us *do* want to take time off to stop and smell the roses. But do you know what keeps us from doing so? It's the people that surround us. Because when everyone around you is rushing to get somewhere, you're bound to wonder whether smelling the roses is such a good idea. You're bound to wonder whether you too would not be better off accomplishing something, rather than letting life just slip by.

'Think about it. The tenets that lead to happiness are no secrets. They're common knowledge in most religions and philosophies. All of us know them well. Why, they're even splattered across calendars in *paan* shops. I guess that's what makes them so corny. I guess that's the reason we're so loathe to try them out. And all I'm doing here Raghu is providing an environment that's conducive to the trying-out.'

'And what happens when the kids pass out of this environment? Wouldn't they eventually be weaned away from— what you call—smelling the roses?' asked Raghu.

It was some time before Abeer answered. 'In Plato's dialogues,' he began, 'when Socrates asks Cephalous—the aristocrat—about the benefits of wealth which he has reaped, Cephalous answers that wealth is what allows him to be honest, and generous, and just. The keyword here is "allows". It shows that Cephalous looks upon honesty, justness and generosity as pleasures; indeed, as a form of lavishness. He doesn't view them as a set of wings that are to fly him into heaven. And that's what smelling the roses is really about. You know Raghu, you can be weaned away from fads; not from things that you've lived and relished—and seen others live and relish—for years together.

'Oh yes! I'm sure my boys will keep riding high; even without the training wheels,' said Abeer.

Training day

On the train journey home, Raghu was lazily ensconced on the side upper berth and reading away the kilometers. Fellow passengers in his cubicle of eight had been found lacking in all variants of audience appeal, which was surprising, because such is usually not the case in second-class compartments. In fact, that tacit conviction was the reason he had chosen to travel in one. He had expected at least one noteworthy episode from the journey. And if his past experience was anything to go by, one episode was something that he could easily take for granted. Of course, the requisite conditions needed to be fulfilled. There had to be at least six hours of day travel in the journey, budding artists were to be provided with due impetus, and one needed to wear the best pair of ears in his wardrobe.

So when the train made its next stop, Raghu knew that it had done so in order to keep the one-episode hypothesis from going awry. And duly, in walked a family of three—Mr Makhija, Mrs Makhija, and twelve-year-old Shammi Makhija. Plump Mrs Makhija was of the school of thought that first impressions are last impressions. She therefore promptly set about getting them right. It was her intention to immediately convey that though she was stranded in a second-class compartment as of now, better modes of travel had been availed by her. Or if not by her, at least by her son Shammi—he of the frowns and raised eyebrows.

MM's first subtle remark, addressed to everybody in general and nobody in particular, was 'How silly of me! Looking for the overhead luggage compartment in a train!' This confession of folly was supposed to be an ice breaker. But from a gang that was low on frequent-flier miles, it failed to elicit any response. MM, who was a seasoned veteran, obviously didn't take the setback to heart. She calmly bided her time. She was well aware of the effect that female strangers can have on the average male traveler. And sure enough, most gazes in the sub-compartment soon turned to her. It was time to hold court. 'Tell me, Shammi,' she asked, as if addressing Shammi on that subject for the very first time, 'what do they do about the unaccompanied luggage in airplanes?' Being adept with his lines, Shammi lowered his brow just the slightest bit and put MM wise on the luggage factor. By the time he was asked about air-hostesses and toilet paper, young Shammi was appropriately warmed up and had duly embarked upon a soliloquy on the merits of air travel.

The conversation so far had been monopolized by the Makhija clan. It hence ran the risk of fizzling away if outside DNA wasn't introduced sometime soon. The onus, Raghu realized, lay solely on him. And hardly had he become aware of this grave responsibility when a cue presented itself in the form of a tea vendor. Raghu, who had been hugely impressed by MM's style of airing questions to thin air, at once used the same approach. 'Is it true that tea and refreshments are free in the airplane?' he inquired of the ceiling fan. Shammi looked up at him and raised his eyebrows, which had drooped considerably by now. 'Yes it's free, but you're charged for it in the ticket.' That lay to rest Raghu's supposed doubts about the philanthropic inclinations of airline owners. Meanwhile, his question had played its role. The henna moustache on seat 47 had now realized that it was okay not to have traveled by plane. He piped in with an air-travel related query which was swiftly quelled satisfactorily. Slanted smile of seat 42 informed everybody about the distant relative who was an air-hostess. The remark was met with all-round general approval. But Mrs Makhija, who abhorred any intrusion into her exclusivity, adroitly ensured that 42 didn't get his full share of glory. She promptly embarked upon a new narrative about the circumstances which had led to young Shammi's plane journey. Apparently, the Makhija lad was good at answering questions—even those that were raised by people other than his mother. The plane ride was part of a prize he had won in a TV quiz-contest.

As the conversation in the sub-compartment began to pick up steam, Raghu contemplated getting down from his berth. The plan was to unobtrusively take a seat amongst Mrs Makhija's enraptured audience. Should things begin to wane, he figured, the new location would be more suited—vis-a-vis his conspicuous perch at the top—for pitching in with the necessary impetus. Yes, it seemed like a good strategic move. But the moment he began his sneaky descent, the bed-linen got caught in his arm and the resulting tug caused the book lying on it to fall onto the floor. It was a hard-cover edition and the thud with which it fell caused everyone to turn with a start. And as if that wasn't enough, Shammi emphatically quashed Raghu's attempt at furtiveness by reading out the embossed words on the book's spine. 'The Barrack-Room Ballads, by Rudyard Kipling,' he said out aloud for the benefit of all.

Raghu hastily picked up the book and flicked away dirt from the pages that had taken the fall. Incidentally, these happened to be the pages that bore the poem 'Gunga Din'; and the words which they first spewed out at him were 'You're a better man than I am, Gunga Din.'

They didn't take long to fall into context, those words. Mesmerized, it was in a zombie-like manner that he walked to his seat in the corner near the aisle. And once seated, it was in a zombie-like manner that he kept staring blankly out of the window. The Makhijas interested him no longer. All he was aware of was an unpleasant feeling in the pit of his stomach.

Did he not indulge in the same tactics as the Makhija lady, he asked himself. Of course, his better education and exposure ensured that his showing-off was of a more sophisticated kind— the 'oh, did it show?' variety. And maybe his affectations were of seemingly greater significance than air travel. But to the trained eye—he realized with unbridled shame—his facades would have appeared as crude and transparent as the ones he had just witnessed. Also, to his better placed audience, his subjects of showing off must have been as trifling as air travel was to him. Hell! What a pathetic picture he must have been to his spectators all these years; a picture rendered all the more ludicrous by the bliss of its own ignorance; a picture not very different from that of the Makhija lady. No, he definitely wasn't the better man here, even though his patronizing was less explicit than that of Kipling.

Raghu felt like throwing up, but ultimately didn't. And MM didn't get to opine on the absence of puke bags in second-class compartments.

Time out

Hardly had Raghu entered his apartment and shut the door behind him when Nandini came rushing and clung to him. It was to be a long hug. As its duration crossed the stipulations of a 'welcome back' and showed no signs of abating even after the full course of 'I missed you so badly' had been run, Raghu surmised that something was the matter. Before long, the wetness on his shoulder provided the confirmation.

'They've gone in for a divorce,' she said at last, between sobs.

'Who?' he asked. Then realizing the question to be redundant, followed it up with another. 'When?'

Nandini went on as if she hadn't heard either. 'It's me, Raghu. I wished it upon them. I had pestered you with that question all the way to Vini's school.' The sobbing was now unrelenting and a good amount of cajoling had to be put in to calm her down. It was a full ten minutes before he could ask 'Who told you about this?'

'Tania did,' she replied.

'Tania?' Raghu started. The two women shared a relationship that just about bordered on the civil. It seemed highly unlikely to him that Tania would call up Nandini to apprise her with news of this sort.

'I met her at Vini's school. She's applying for a job there.'

'C'mon. Abhay couldn't have left her that high and dry.'

'He didn't. Tanya says he's been very generous on that account. He's given her an open ended offer for the alimony.'

'And Tania isn't taking it?'

'No.'

'But when did all this happen? Is it actually legal or is it just talk between them?' he wanted to know.

'About a week back. The judge has ordered a year of separation before he puts a stamp on it. She's moved in with her parents for now.'

Raghu became quiet. There were many questions in his mind but they were all addressed to Abhay.

'I still feel somewhat responsible for this,' said Nandini at length, as she managed to wring out the last two tears.

Nandini's unfounded guilt was merely an excuse which her subconscious had concocted for her near hysteria. It was the divorce, and not the victims' plight, which had shaken her. Because even though they're known to all, it's only in the wake of an accident involving a kin that the perils of hasty driving become truly apparent.

Raghu tried getting in touch with Abhay but found his cellphone unreachable. Then upon contacting Abhay's office, he got to know that Abhay was out of the country and would remain so for the next fortnight. He deliberately didn't ask for an interim contact number. Had Abhay so intended, figured Raghu, he would have left instructions for him to be notified. Abhay's need for solitude was understandable and Raghu let it be.

The days that followed saw the emotions at the Kumar's abate a bit. Raghu drove with more awareness, and Nandini gave up her habit of abrupt clutch-release and unnecessary honking.

Another development was the Nandini-Tania proximity. Since Tania had bagged the teaching job and because Vini needed to be picked up from school every weekday, the two ladies got to see a lot of each other. Affinity grew and Tania often came to visit the Kumar residence.

Raghu was lazing on the living room rug with Vini, a box of Lego between them, when Nandini walked in.

'Vini tells me that Tania Aunty is coming...again,' said Raghu with a little smirk. Of course, he had nothing against Nandini's new found affection for Tania. He in fact even thought it beneficial for a possible Abhay-Tania patch-up. But there was no harm in some good-natured leg pulling, especially if it also drove home a point.

'I wonder why people get facelifts and expensive cars to make themselves more popular. Shouldn't they should just go and buy a new misfortune?' he continued.

'Shut up, Raghu,' said Nandini good humouredly. 'You know that hasn't got much to do with it.'

'Really?'

'It's just that I had never known her that well.'

'Understandable. The glitter from her designer diamonds must've impeded your view. Or shall we say, refracted it?'

Nandini was just about to hurl a magazine at him when the bell rang. It was Tania.

'Hi Raghu,' she greeted. 'Nice to see you back early from work.'

'Wisdom from Himachal!' said Nandini. She hadn't meant to let that escape but could not resist the temptation to retaliate.

'No it's not,' lied Raghu reflexively.

'Then?' pressed Nandini.

'Tell us,' joined in Tania.

Thus cornered, he needed to come up with some sort of a plausible reply. Plain evasion would have been tantamount to confirming the schoolboy embarrassment that had caused him to lie. And no man wants to appear an embarrassed schoolboy to a beautiful woman.

'Uhh...it's something from my Scad days,' he began, trying to sound very casual.

'I'm all ears,' mocked Nandini.

'In Scad, during examination time, I was always the last boy to leave the prep room. I mean, irrespective of whether I'd finished my revision or not, I'd just keep sitting there. It made me feel insecure to leave if any of my classmates was still studying.'

'So?'

'So I've decided it's high time I dropped that habit.' And Kalra could go to hell, he wanted to add.

'Clap, clap,' said Nandini. Though she half believed him, she was keen that the matter be dismissed as a joke. She had as yet not asked Raghu why he had taken to coming home on time. This wasn't because she lacked curiosity. But like any sensible woman, she was content with the fruit. Counting the trees whence it came held the danger of stirring a hornet's nest.

'Ah, I almost forgot,' she said. 'Let me get you people something to drink.'

Nandini took her time to fetch the drinks and the awkwardness between the stranded pair only intensified with each passing moment. When the wife of one's best friend has gone and asked the best friend for a divorce, there's hardly any small talk that can be made with her. Even an innocuous comment on the weather stands to be misconstrued. Raghu knew that he was very likely to make a *faux pas* if he so much as opened his mouth. He chose not to and the pregnant silence continued to fester. Then finally, drinks were delivered.

'What juice is this Papa?' asked Vini.

'Orange, *beta*,' replied Raghu.

'But I want apple juice,' she demanded. Having been deprived of attention for so long, she considered it her right to throw a tantrum.

'But *beta*, it isn't the season for apples yet,' implored Raghu. The Kumars were fresh-juice enthusiasts.

Vini let out a loud wail. She despised being pacified with such incomprehensible adult prattle. To yield to it would have been a blot upon her intelligence.

'All right, all right,' stepped in Nandini when the wail showed no sign of abating. 'Now be a good girl and tell aunty when your birthday is.'

'Seventh July,' replied Vini, perhaps in the hope of an early present.

'You see, just as you have *your* birthday, all fruits have *their* birthdays. Just like you are happiest during your birthday, all fruits are happiest during the month of *their* birthdays. That's when they allow you to squeeze them for some juice. This is the month of Orange's birthday. Three months from now, we'll have Apple's birthday. That's when we'll request Apple for some juice. Right now, I think we should all wish Orange a happy birthday and drink up.'

'Happy birthday, Orange,' said the three adults.

'Happy birthday, Orange,' mumbled Vini, as she took a reluctant sip.

'That was good,' whispered Tania to Nandini.

Raghu was smiling. 'What?' asked Nandini.

'Nothing,' he replied.

When the two ladies had left, he was telling Vini, 'You know Vini, Uncle Truth is always so willing to come to the party. What a shame that he seldom knows what set of words to wear to which.'

Being the lone audience, Vini felt it obligatory to giggle at the joke.

Homeward bound

Abhay caught up on a little breakfast as he waited for his flight home. The week-long trip had turned out to be a tedious one, even though work had originally been a mere pretext for the journey. His real intention had been to spend some time alone. It was his belief that solitude would have the same effect on his thoughts that immobility and time have upon muddy waters. Unfortunately, the only solitude he got was in airplane seats and hotel beds. It proved to be inadequate. And the waters remained as they were.

His lazily perambulating gaze was now entangled among a couple of female flight-attendants. As he looked at their painted lips, rouged cheeks, mascaraed lashes, and perfectly done hair, he couldn't help thinking of Tania in the context; about how fond she was of all such adornments, and the amount of time she spent on them before going out to a social do. And how he absolutely hated it all.

The adornments, by themselves, were not an aggravation. What rendered them repugnant were the plastic smile and the affected voice that came alongside. Together, they constituted an appalling mix which to Abhay was a manifestation of that one thing which he abhorred most—shallowness.

But that was not all. Because just as a chain is judged by its weakest link, an individual is judged by the most tarnished spot on her personality; or more accurately, by what her fellow beings *consider* to be the most tarnished spot on her personality. And expectedly, in the face of the tarnished spot, any praiseworthy qualities which she might possess are righteously relegated to oblivion. Abhay therefore could never bring himself to connect with Tania. Her act during their societal outings left behind a taste too sour for his sensitive mouth. What made matters worse was the fact that Tania would rarely let up on the act even when the event was over. It was probably the momentum from being the party's centre of attraction. Or maybe, it was her way to assert that the put-on was not really a put-on, and that she was in that 'mood' for the entire evening. Whatever might have been the reason, the end result remained the same: there was more sour taste to contend with. Poor Tania found it baffling and slighting and, eventually, exasperating.

The highs and lows of matrimony simply did not happen. And stripped of the potential difference of highs and lows, the marriage was stripped too of the energy which triggers domestic detonation. It was therefore a whimper, and not a bang, with which their bond ruptured.

Tania paid the price for playing by the rules of a game she had been thrust into. As for her husband, what he bore was purely the brunt of an idiosyncrasy.

Abhay's sullen gaze had meandered back and it now rested on his empty cup. There was still much time left for the flight home.

Suddenly, a distantly familiar voice spoke, 'Is that the purveyor of good spirits, or do my old eyes deceive me?'

'Aari,' said Abhay, not quite with the fervor or surprise that is characteristic of such occasions.

'Of course it is I. And Mnemosyne be praised that you recall!'

'It wasn't difficult. You've hardly aged. Silicon Valley has been taking good care of you it seems.'

'I guess I'm compelled to agree. Those valleys of silicon, in all their voluptuous splendour, have indeed been a deterrent to my aging process.'

'You definitely haven't changed,' smiled Abhay.

Aari pulled up a chair and sat himself down. But what endured for the next few minutes was an awkward silence. Abhay was not one to start a conversation, or to keep one going. He simply allowed the hush to persist.

'Met Raghu recently?' was what Aari eventually came up with. After all, that was their common bond.

'About three weeks back,' was the reply.

'Had a talk with him yesterday,' volunteered Aari, 'we're meeting over the weekend.'

Abhay nodded a smile.

'That's the thing about America,' continued Aari. 'It makes you really appreciative of friends back home.'

'So after *Sleepless in Seattle* we have *Solitary in Silicon Valley*.'

'Oh yes, it does get lonely here. But it's nowhere as bad as it was in the beginning.'

Abhay looked at Aari with a start. What little he knew of Aari, he hadn't expected him to take his remark at face value and continue on that lead.

'You wouldn't believe,' went on Aari in a matter of fact manner, 'how I spent my meager allowance during my early days here.'

'The peep shows?' Abhay was determined to keep the conversation from turning sentimental.

'Something equally obscene. I used to call up Raghu the pig. And mind you, I was really short on cash those days. Now add to that Raghu's penchant for the line "a good friend is one with whom you can share comfortable silences." Yesssss, but for heaven sake, not on international calls!

'The silence of the pig served to silence my piggy bank for good. Gradually, I stopped calling.'

'In other words, you simply got used to the loneliness.'

'You can say that. But more importantly, I believe I realized something.'

'And that was?' It wasn't inquisitiveness. The question had slipped out in reflex.

'That we over-romanticize the concept of "people like us".'

'Come again!'

'You know, the bunch from college or school who we spent our youth hanging out with; the people who would burst into laughter at that exact moment in *Get Shorty*; the people who had surprisingly similar taste buds, be it in music, denims, or integrity; and perhaps most important of all, the people who more or less had the same levels of respect—for self and for authority.

'Not that we didn't allow these people their individuality. All were fiercely individualistic. And yet when it came to the basic stances, all had their melting and boiling points set in the same range.'

'And you're still telling me not to over-romanticize the concept?'

'Yes. Because the point to ponder is, how did these people come about? I met Raghu and Abeer by sheer chance on the first day in the institute. And today I realize that despite our disparate nature, we almost always concur on things that matter. Sheer coincidence? I would think not.

'Neither was I like them to begin with, nor were they like me. Then as we spent our important formative years together, we unconsciously kept borrowing from each other. Or rather, kept borrowing from that which could be referred to as the "highest common factor"—and sometimes, the "lowest common multiple"—of the pool.'

'Pool!'

'The pool of common personality—to which we all contributed and from which we all drank! Drank that near same water and drank it for years together. No surprise then that we're all "people like us".'

'Just because you can explain it doesn't mean that you can escape it. Besides, why would you want to escape that which you are?'

'Because that's not what I necessarily am. Had I drunk from a different pool, I would have been *that*. So why should I be stuck with the personality of my youth? Or more importantly, why should I ever get stuck at all. Raghu and Abeer are wonderful people. I really value and relish their friendship. But that doesn't mean the parts of personality I picked up in their company should be used to judge others. You can't go through life with a slipper in hand, seeking out the Cinderella whom that slipper once fitted.'

'But suppose there actually is a Cinderella,' said Abhay after a brief pause. 'Don't you believe in a soulmate?'

'Soulmate, my foot. That's the only mate my sole has. Whoever came up with that term must have been a crooked genius. Soulmate! The best excuse for dissatisfaction in a relationship. A real crafty escape mechanism.'

'And you of all people object to that?'

'I, of all people, object to that because I've taken undue advantage of that excuse. Never stuck around with a woman once her charm wore off. Not for me the *working* on a relationship.

Simply replaced the car when the glaze lessened, or when the shock absorbers gave me the slightest trouble. In short, never got around to the maintenance stage.

'What's more, not once did I feel guilty. Rationalization always rode on the thought that wearing off wouldn't have happened if she were "the one". But "the one" never came and wearing off never ceased. Would you believe it, I once broke up with a dame—just couldn't bring myself to go on really—simply because I'd heard her fart.'

Very imperceptibly, Abhay smiled. And it wasn't at the flippancy of what he'd heard.

'Well actually it's not as absurd it sounds. This lady I talk of was all about dignity. Dignity was her USP and dignity is what lent sheen to her charisma. Then like a bolt from the blue came this fart. I tell you, that sound was the death knell of our relationship. Brought her whole persona crashing down. Yes, I was being unreasonable. Yes, people fart. I fart. Farts are no reason to break up with people. But the thing is that there is not much you can do about whims and fancies. Schopenhauer is so right when he talks about *Will*—that strong blind man who carries little lame intellect on his shoulders. Like he says, we will not understand because we *will* not understand.'

Abhay's smile broadened. His otherwise inert *will* had just made some stirring sounds that chimed of a strange amity. And though he was at first puzzled as to how this phenomenon had come about under such ordinary circumstances, memories from an afternoon gone by made it clear. A few months back he'd taken Vini to a fair and—while giving in to the child's wishes— had landed up inside a house of distorted mirrors. One of the ludicrous reflections which had caught the child's fancy was that of him with a ballooned stomach. She had laughed harder than usual upon seeing it. He had laughed too. And as the two of them were lost in that easy pleasure, the image drove home a point which repeated hints from kinfolk had failed to deliver. It at once made him cognizant of the extra pounds he had put on.

Abhay had done it that afternoon and he couldn't help do it now; he marveled. He marveled at how naked facts could stare one in the face 24/7 and still not crystallize into a revelation; and how those crystallizations could be facilitated by certain catalysts; and that the catalyst called 'exaggeration' happened to be a universal hit.

He smiled sardonically at his own thoughts and that derision—inadvertently—seeped through to his remark as well. 'So, you in the maintenance mood now?' he asked.

A lesser soul would have been hushed into reticence by that sneer. But Aari was by no means a lesser soul. Besides, he was simply too overwhelmed from his recent brush with a serendipitous insight. His was a joy that cried out to be shared. And Abhay, who embodied that right mix of trustworthiness and detachment, qualified as a perfect receptacle.

'Yes, maintenance's the reason I'm off to Delhi,' replied Aari.

'And what brings the change of heart?'

'Time, I think. You know, I'm kind of getting over the hill. Tastes have changed. Perspectives have changed. Pleasures that once tickled don't do so now. And....and I really think I love her. But to be honest, there's a reason why that realization has so suddenly dawned. Yup! She's the kind of person to walk out on me before *I* do. Besides, I'm getting over the hill. Damn! Now I'm repeating myself. But you do get the basic picture, don't you? C'mon, there are so many movies on this stuff. Pick anything with Jack Nicholson in it.'

Abhay laughed aloud. He also reached out for the coffee pot.

There was this spontaneous urge to fill the empty cup.

Abhay was back in town and Raghu was afflicted with this childish urge of surprising him with an unannounced visit. Also, for childish urges rarely do singly come, Raghu found himself yielding to impatience. So what was supposed to be a dinnertime call to Abhay's house turned into an early-evening visit to his office. Raghu, while driving home from work, impulsively took a detour.

It didn't take long for him to regret his decision. His host happened to be away and wasn't expected back for at least an hour. Raghu considered leaving but since the detour he'd taken wasn't a minor one, he decided to wait it out.

Not long after he had made himself comfortable in the waiting lounge, Richa—Abhay's secretary—turned up. As expected, their conversation kicked off with some customary small talk. Then after it had exhausted the initial surge, it tottered down the trail of platitudes. All turn of dialogue was determined by the typecast image that each carried of the other. And soon a conversation that so easily could have been perfectly robust stood gasping for every exchange. By the end, Richa offered Raghu the use of Abhay's personal chamber. He would be more comfortable there, she suggested. Raghu politely declined. Knowing that he would do so with the proffered beverage as well, Richa refrained from asking his preference and—as she left the lounge—asked for some coffee to be sent over to him. Predictably, he accepted it.

The coffee was good. It always was at Abhay's office. But instead of simply relishing the coffee, Raghu got wondering why its taste varied so much from kitchen to kitchen. It surprised him that a thing with just four ingredients could be concocted in that many flavours. He tried to do some math using those four parameters, but the answers yielded by the theory of permutations seemed incongruous with the facts. Then suddenly, it occurred to him that 'cooking temperature' was a parameter too; and he instantly set about doing the math again, this time also factoring in 'point in time when an ingredient was added' as a variable. But the whole thing got too complicated and he let it go.

And with that letting go arrived a waft of ironic awareness. He realized how effortlessly he'd been able to comprehend the extent of complexity in an item comprising only four ingredients; and yet when it came to humans, that same assessment did not as easily happen. The full extent of human complexity became apparent to him only now. And only now did he start to see the folly behind typecasting and categorizing people. Not surprisingly, what followed in the wake of his realization was a feeling of mild excitement. He at once wanted to put to test his insight. He wanted to have a whole new conversation with Richa. But prudence came to prevail in the nick of time and he abandoned the idea.

Raghu smiled at his own impetuousness as he leaned back in his chair. Then he tilted his head to one side and shut his eyes; not so much to lull himself into sleep as to acknowledge the long hour which needed to be whiled away. Expectedly, it was only a matter of seconds before he reached out for his mobile phone. But hardly had he got a hold on the instrument when he checked himself. He had suddenly been reminded of something which Abeer had said. 'Do you know why the smartphone is such a huge success? It's a contraption that assists you in keeping you away from yourself. What's more, it provides you with guilt-free reasons for avoiding that meeting. No single device in history has pulled off that stunt so effectively.' It wasn't as if Raghu hadn't realized the veracity of that statement the first time over. Just that he'd skipped over it abruptly and not given it enough time to sink in. But now, for absolutely no particular reason at all, the whole thing began to seem very pertinent. Indeed—realized Raghu—when having a snack, while waiting for someone, during travel, and even in the loo, he was unrelentingly fidgeting with his phone and reading up even the most inane of scraps which it hurled at him. 'Don't be so scared to be with yourself,' Abeer had urged. 'You'd be surprised at the things that the you is trying to tell you. Learn to listen to the you. It's like a child. You never know what'll cause it to open up to you, but yes, one ingredient of that recipe is time. Spend time with it.'

In saying no to the phone Raghu was paying heed to those words. Also, 'it' had finally been granted an appointment. The two of them now sat in silence and stared blankly at the wall. But belying his expectations, no movie played out on the screen of his mind. He stared some more. Still no movie. Perhaps it took time and practice, he consoled himself. Yet refuge in the phone he did not take.

Then when he least expected them, they came. Thoughts. Unstructured and disarrayed. Thoughts of Abhay as a kid in Scad, thoughts of Abhay at the helm of his empire. Thoughts of Tania as he'd come to know her now, thoughts of Nandini as he'd known her *then*. Thoughts of Vini and her vulnerability, thoughts of his own childhood. Thoughts of Abhay again. Thoughts that made him all the more determined for the task he had cut out for himself—the task of threshing out with Abhay this matter of the divorce and the sell-off. He had evaded the issue long enough. At first for fear of galvanizing a decision. And now—when all the decisions had actually been taken—for fear of making a fool of himself. After all, how does one offer advice to somebody who's been far more successful than oneself? And always! But Raghu had made up his mind. He would do it. Despite all the risk to his self esteem, he would definitely do it.

As he sat reeling under the weight of his altruism, little did Raghu Kumar realize that he was being watched. Abhay stood on the other side of the glass door, staring at him fixedly.

Abhay's attention had instantly been caught by Raghu's wall wall-staring posture the moment he'd entered the office. Then by and by, the reverie he witnessed turned contagious and he too was prompted into one of his own. He now dwelled among the childhood and teenage days that he and Raghu had spent together. The passing years had seen the two of them undergo many changes. And yet, the cord that bound them had remained much the same. How gratifying it was, he reflected, to have at least a few constant things in life. He had heard it said that a friend is best judged by his attitude during one's trying times. He wondered whether the diametrically opposite wasn't true as well. Was not the attitude of a friend during one's unexpectedly fortunate times a better test of his character?

Eventually, a small stir in the office caused both trances to break. Their gazes fell on each other almost simultaneously, and Raghu thought it odd that Abhay's smile of acknowledgement should be wider than usual.

'How was your visit to the hills?' asked Abhay as they took chairs in his chamber.

'Nice. But how do *you* know about it?' countered Raghu.

'I too intend to meet Abeer one of these days.'

Though that was not an answer to his question, Raghu let it go. He however didn't fail to notice the ghost of a smirk which had flitted across Abhay's face.

'What are you waiting for then?' asked Raghu.

'An avalanche perhaps,' answered Abhay after some thought.

'At this time of the year?'

'Never rule out an avalanche,' replied Abhay. And before Raghu could ask him to elaborate, he continued, 'Guess what? I met Aari.'

'Aari Ghosh?'

'The very same.'

'How's he?'

'Seems fine. Has also made peace with his illustrious elder brother.'

'I guess that was bound to happen. His brother's nowhere as despicable as his achievements make him out to be.'

'Now why do I sense that that barb is not entirely aimed at Aari's brother?' Abhay smiled.

'Why indeed?' countered Raghu with a sly grin.

'C,mon, give it to me straight. You needn't bend stuff with me.'

'The bending thing is best left to Beckham. Why would *I* indulge in an uphill task like that?' Hardly had he said that when something amusing struck him. Amid a snigger, he continued 'Talking of hills and Beckham, there is this soccer question you might want to answer.'

'Shoot.'

Raghu paused for a moment—like one does before a free kick—before he asked, 'Tell me, why did George Mallory kick the football?'

'Is there a parable in that riddle?' queried Abhay.

'Maybe. Say, why did George Mallory kick the football?'

'Because it was there?' replied Abhay after some thought.

'Exactly. Because it was there. But just because things are there, just because *everything* is there doesn't imply that we kick them away.'

Abhay laughed. 'I see that cutting down on work is doing wonders for your sensahuma.'

'Who told you about my cutting down on work?'

'Well, perhaps I'm not doing as much kicking as you attribute to me.'

'Hell!' said Raghu with a start 'You met Tania!'

Abhay smiled in reply.

The joy on Raghu's face was palpable. 'When? Where?' he managed to ask, as a rush of emotions threatened to turn the conversation incoherent.

'Half an hour back. Had coffee together.'

'And?'

'And what?'

'And what happened. Tell me all.'

'We talked about stuff. You and Nandini among other things.'

'Forget me and Nandini. Tell me the pertinent part.'

'I reminded her of the judge's order. Told her that the year he's given us is for us to reconsider our decision. And that if we didn't do so, he could well hold us in contempt of court.'

Raghu laughed. Abhay too conceded a smile.

'You reminded her of the judge's order!' said Raghu from between his laugh, 'What else did you remind her of?'

'Hopefully, not myself,' was the wistful reply.

Raghu took Abhay home for dinner. This evening too, he didn't touch upon Abhay's business sell-off plans. Commerce and industry couldn't be allowed to sully the clear stream.

Look who's coming to dinner

Brinda and Aari were coming over for dinner and Nandini was more than a little flustered about the evening that lay ahead. She had been that way ever since she'd heard Menaaz inquire with raised eyebrows, '*The* Brinda Nadar?'

'You know her?' had been Nandini's anxious counter-question.

'Who doesn't?'

'And may I know how?'

'The same way Helen Keller got purple fingers—listening to the grape-wine.'

Nandini tried to laugh but it came out all jittery. Notoriety always made her uncomfortable.

'Actually,' continued Menaaz, 'most of what I've heard about her is from a cousin who is a fashion-designer. He says that people simply hate her guts. She's rich, she's beautiful, and she's intelligent. Besides, she *knows* she is all that. And as if that wasn't bad enough, her father happens to hail from a family of old money, and her mother belongs to one that boasts of at least two poets and a painter.'

'Ah! So no burden of pretensions to cultured affluence.'

'Precisely,' nodded Menaaz, 'She was there for Pavarotti's last performance in Turin and claimed not to like it. To the question "How can you *not* like the tenor?" she'd coolly replied "Because

I can afford not to".'

'So she's witty too.'

'But without affiliations to any style. If Rohit—my cousin—is to be believed, her wit can be terse and dry and caustic. Also, it can be wet and syrupy and elaborate—something in which she marinates her prey for an entire evening before going for the final slash.'

'C'mon, you're scaring me.'

'On the plus side, Rohit says that *he* could never come up with a reason to dislike her. She's just different. And perhaps, also a bit strange.'

'How different and how strange—I guess I'll find out soon enough,' Nandini consoled herself.

What Nandini *did* find out was that Brinda was nothing like the wild child image of hers that she'd conjured up. She was quick to identify the error that had led to it. When Menaaz had described Brinda, Nandini had simply gone along with the first draft of the character sketch that her imagination had served up. She had even assigned certain facial features and a certain gait to Brinda. That sketch, she now realized, was just one of the many options which fitted the description. For it was possible for Brinda to be all those things which Menaaz had said *and* not be a wild child. Then again, by judging Brinda so soon, she was perhaps falling prey to that other common error—of allowing appearances, and first ones at that, to deceive her. For all she knew, Brinda could yet be the wild child that didn't come in a standard wild-child packing.

She abruptly weaned herself away from her murky train of thought and set about making her guests feel at home. Thankfully, Aari was as uncomplicated and boisterous as ever.

'Macallan,' he said, picking up one of the bottles laid out at the bar, 'Bacchus be praised, it's a single-single! I think I'm going to drink like a fish tonight. Hope you have enough of this stuff.'

'Enough to stuff you to the gills,' replied Raghu.

'Pity that the fish turns out to be a red herring,' smiled Brinda, 'the man's been a teetotaler for about two years now.'

Raghu turned towards Aari with a bewildered expression. What he'd heard was hard for him to believe.

'The exile's self imposed,' came the defense, 'There's nothing that prevents me from walking out of it, if only for this one time.'

'But why?' persisted Raghu, 'why in the first place did you do it?' It was inconceivable to him that Aari should give up a sensory pleasure. And that too of his own volition!

Aari hedged away the question with an innocuous digression. 'You look absolutely ravishing Nandini. Seem even prettier than you did four years back.'

'Weren't you supposed to say that the moment you entered?' countered Nandini. This wasn't the sort of retort that Aari had expected. He had anticipated some fumbled thanking accompanied by awkward attempts to return the compliment. However, none of it really mattered. The remark had served its purpose and the conversation stood deflected. Aari answered Nandini with an inane wisecrack and the banter veered towards healthy small talk.

'I was looking forward to meet you,' said Brinda to Raghu

'You don't have to be so formal,' he quipped.

Brinda smiled. This was obviously an allegation that had never been leveled upon her.

'No seriously,' she said, 'you know that *dosti* kind of friendship typical of the subcontinent? I thing you're his only *dost*. And hence I was keen to meet you.'

Raghu was taken aback. The thought that Aari viewed him

in such light had never actually occurred to him; not only because he didn't reciprocate the feeling with the same intensity, but also because he had never considered Aari capable of such emotions. It was to ward off his embarrassment that he spoke. 'Talking of meetings, I'm kind of keen to know how *you* guys met.'

The moment was awkward. Aari looked towards Brinda with something that was almost akin to trepidation. Whenever questions that bordered on the personal had been asked of her on previous occasions, the inquirer had either been ignored or unceremoniously ticked off. Attempting an answer—even an evasive one—was to Brinda the equivalent of allowing entry into private territory. And she was very intolerant of trespassers.

But looking at the expression on her face now, Aari relaxed. There was no need for him to intervene. Brinda Nadar was about to make an exception.

'Serendipity,' she replied, 'I was the proverbial bitch and he was the much celebrated bastard. When two of those get into the same town, I guess they are fated to meet.'

Nandini almost coughed out her drink. A hurried apology followed. 'It was too cold. And I have these really sensitive molars. I think they're rotting or something.'

'I wonder,' started Aari, primarily to puncture the awkward silence that had trailed Nandini's feeble alibi, 'what if *I* had rotting teeth. Would that make my bark worse than my bite?'

'But where in the first place does your bark get into the picture? You're merely the bastard, remember. It is *I* who is supposed to be the bitch,' countered Brinda, 'unless of course you happen to be making a formal proposal.'

'Well if that's what it is,' quipped Aari, 'the first thing I need to know is how many knees proposing canines go down on.'

'Shove it. Just raise a leg and take a leak,' joined in Raghu, 'stick to things you've always been good at.'

Brinda laughed out loud. Apparently, taking leaks was something she was pretty good at too.

As the evening progressed and the cogs of conversation got better lubricated with alcohol and renewed memories, it emerged that the couple had another quality in common: ennui. The thin crust of ebullience couldn't for long conceal the intense boredom which festered underneath. It was understandable. They had in the prime of their youth been blessed with resources and attributes far greater than are necessary for a life of complete hedonism. And they had in accordance with those blessings savored all conceivable pleasures that came their way; savored them to an extent greater than satiety, and with an intensity that was sufficient to blunt the senses.

For individuals burnt out in this fashion, there was little left to do but to raise legs and take leaks at the vestiges of their indulgences. Indeed, Brinda was doing just that.

'Getting rid of desire isn't the problem. At least not as big as GB makes it out to be,' she declared.

'GB?' asked Raghu.

'Gautam Buddha.'

'Ah!' exclaimed Raghu, and after a moment added, 'Do go on. Tell us. How does one succeed where most of GB's disciples fail?'

'By overindulgence,' answered Brinda calmly. 'For getting around desire, I would strongly recommend overindulgence. Overindulgence is the systematic method for putting out an oil-well fire. You kill the fire by starving it of its oxygen supply by means of an engineered explosion. So you see, overindulgence is fun, and the learning it begets is somewhat more permanent and authentic. Take your *dost's* example. He started his career in debauchery with an obsession for great pairs of tits. When he tired of them, he graduated to great tits that were affixed beneath a smart head. What naturally followed were small tits and a smart head.'

'Is that around the time you guys met?'

'No, but your subtlety is much appreciated. Anyway, coming back to your question, by the time *we* met he had moved on to some really nuanced and refined fetishes. And after that there wasn't all that much left to explore. A dead end stared him in the face.'

'But he could always go back to step one again. I'm sure the great pairs would have regained some of their lost charm. It would've been like exploring new territory.'

'Quite right. But only quite. Because the problem with second rounds is that stored memories get in the way. If the first tour took him, say, three years to complete, the second round—depending upon his intelligence—would take him anything between three weeks to three months.'

'Are you sure of that?'

Brinda's answer was a smile. It was not meant to be a supercilious one, but there was little she could do to prevent it from looking that way.

'Have you heard about Voltaire's good Brahmin?' she asked.

Raghu shook his head and Brinda continued, 'It's a story Voltaire tells about a learned Brahmin. Full of doubts, the Brahmin's a man in misery. He has spent forty years studying the sacred texts but all in vain. His confusion about existence has only intensified with the passing years. What's more, that confusion isn't confined to existential angst alone. A plethora of other questions are forever bombarding him. What produces thought? Is understanding a simple faculty like walking or digestion? Does the head grasp ideas the way a hand grasps an object? The Brahmin's a man all at sea.

'Conversely, an old woman who lives nearby goes about happily with her simple life. Not for her any questions about the nature of soul and existence. She simply doesn't comprehend them. She believes in the incarnations of Vishnu and is ecstatic if she's able to obtain for her ablutions some water from the holy Ganges.

'Is he not aware of this woman's existence, the Brahmin is asked. He is, he answers. Is he then not aware of her happiness? He is too, he replies. "But that is not a kind of happiness I would desire for myself," he solemnly adds.'

'Hardly a good Brahmin,' said Raghu after a short silence. 'Seemed rather conceited to me.'

Brinda laughed. 'Surprising that the conceit thing never struck me in all these years. But I guess that's because I don't mind conceit that's legitimate. Anyway, the issue is not conceit. The issue is the correlation between our happiness and our levels of awareness. The old woman is happier than the good Brahmin because her levels of awareness are lesser than his.'

'So what Voltaire's saying is that knowledge doesn't liberate, and that it in fact enslaves.'

'Up to a point, yes. Because the correlation between knowledge and happiness dots out an inverted parabola curve. Call it the bucket curve if you will. When we start from our initial position of innocence, all awareness that we gain only serves to lessen our happiness. Happiness goes on a free-fall decline till it hits rock-bottom. Then from that point onwards, knowledge does a role reversal. Hereafter, each enhancement in knowledge brings about an enhancement in consolation and joy. But the truth is that by the time we arrive at this bottom of the parabola, most of us have already given up on knowledge.

Further, to make matters worse, gravity ensures that we remain forever trapped at the bottom—that bottom of least happiness.'

'And maximum apparent stability.'

'And maximum apparent stability,' echoed Brinda.

'In that case, it obviously makes more sense to stay like the old woman, to not take that first step towards awareness.'

'Yes it does. But the important point—the point that Voltaire forgets to mention—is that those steps towards awareness are not in our control. You must remember that the old woman is able to stay in that state only because hers is an isolated world; whereas for most of us, increasing awareness is not a choice but a natural fallout of going about our day to day business. Successive layers of our innocence get punctured with each passing experience. And sadly, that's an irreversible process. A layer once punctured can never be repaired. I hate to say it but five years hence, your wonderfully happy daughter won't have her existing levels of glee.'

'Which is also the reason that though there might be a short-lived second round for Aari, there definitely isn't going to be a third one.'

'But debauchery isn't the only distraction. He can easily switch over to money, power, fame.'

'They're only worse. They don't even allow for a second round. The moment you cross a level, you become immune to that degree of potency for life.'

'Are you always this depressing?'

'As I was saying, getting rid of desire isn't as difficult as it's touted to be. What's *difficult*—once you've given up desire—is to get up the next morning and have something to do.'

Raghu smiled. It had come to his notice that Brinda was sitting in the same chair that Abhay had occupied a few days back.

Brinda, meanwhile, went on undeterred, 'What do you do with a car when the engine has stalled? Because that's exactly what desires are—engines that power our lives.'

'I guess that makes morals and values the steering mechanism,' put in Nandini.

'I guess it does,' replied Brinda.

'And what's your opinion on tacky steering wheels?'

Brinda did not take offense. She in fact smiled before she answered, 'They result in some wrong turns. And wrong turns show us some really beautiful countryside.'

Even Nandini couldn't suppress a little laugh.

It was very late in the night when they sat down to dinner. And the only reason they did so was that no one wanted to be discourteous to Nandini's efforts. 'I think Brinda has spilled them all,' said Aari, 'but if there are any left, please pass the beans.'

Soft focus, high resolution

Abeer and Raghu sat eating parathas at the IIT hostel gate *dhaba*. Abeer was in Delhi for some official work and the pleasure trip to IIT was meant as compensation for the hard day he'd had at the government offices.

'Chai?' asked Chhotu the waiter.

'Nah. *Nimbu pani*,' replied Raghu.

The *nimbu pani* that eventually arrived apprised Raghu of the chef's shedding condition. Raghu politely asked Chhotu to replace his drink. Abeer laughed out loud.

'What?' asked Raghu.

Abeer wouldn't stop laughing.

'What?' repeated Raghu. 'What's so funny about a hair floating in the *nimbu pani*?'

'Your voluntarily asking for Chhotu's grimy finger to retrieve it,' was the answer.

Raghu smiled at his own foolishness. He had *actually* expected a replacement. 'What's it with optimism and this campus?' he mumbled to himself. But the words didn't escape Abeer. Also, since Abeer's expression was a clear giveaway that he understood whom the remark referred to, Raghu scurried to change the subject. 'Wouldn't you like to meet Abhay?' he asked, as he politely refused the *nimbu pani* from the sheepishly smiling Chhotu.

'But I *am* meeting him for the whole of tomorrow. That's the main reason I'm here. Didn't Abhay tell you?' asked Abeer.

'Tell me what?'

'About his charitable trust—the one that's funded by his phased business disinvestments.'

'Go on.'

'He intends the trust to take up subsidized education. He says he likes the prototype in Niranjanpur.'

It took Raghu a while to absorb the information. 'The bastard,' he said smiling 'So that's what he meant by an avalanche.'

'Oh yes, the quantum's pretty substantial. He's disinvested from his overseas ventures as well.'

They walked around the campus feeding on sparse conversation. Then as they passed their old hostel the second time, Abeer let out nostalgically, 'Those were the days! Not a care in the world.'

'Not a care in the world?' objected Raghu. 'Talk to any of those kids rushing to the library. They'll remind you of all the cares we had.'

'Granted. But even adjusting for the retrospect factor—that distorter of experience—I would still say they were great days. And c'mon, you for one shouldn't be refuting that.'

Raghu sensed where Abeer was headed. 'I'm not exactly denying…' he fumbled.

'But neither do you seem to agree.'

Raghu chose to be quiet. And once again, it was Abeer who broke the silence 'Think about it. Which do you suppose was the happiest period of your life?'

'Difficult to put a finger on,' replied Raghu at length. 'Vini's birth perhaps.'

'Happiest period I ask, not happiest moment.'

'Okay, it was those carefree IIT days, if that's what you're trying to get at.'

'I'm not trying to get at anything. You're trying to get *away* from something. And for the second time this evening.'

They walked some more before Raghu confessed, 'You're probably right. She *was* the happiest period of my life.'

'Are you scared to say the name? Scared that it'll rekindle some of those feelings?'

'What exactly are you trying to do? Disgruntle my marriage?' asked Raghu jovially.

'I'm just asking you to say a name.'

'Lila,' said Raghu after a small silence, which had apparently been employed to quarantine the name from the rest of the conversation. 'Lila,' he repeated. It felt good to roll the tongue around that sound.

'You just had to say it one time. First love, by its very definition, is a one-time phenomenon,' said Abeer. It was in a mock dreamy demeanour that he added, 'I distinctly remember that one year. You spent it in a single pair of shoes. Walking on air hardly causes any wear and tear you see. Then there were your cheek muscles—perpetually strained by pulling up the lip corners into a moronic smile. Man, if your affair would have lasted even a month longer, those muscles would have perished with fatigue. Mention must also be...'

Raghu cut him short. 'Okay! I get the general idea. So yes, happiness peaked around that time. But what's your point?'

'My point is that it did so for a reason. Happiness peaked because it's always in direct proportion to the amount of love that you hold. And hence by corollary, in inverse proportion to the hatred that you carry.'

'Ah! Love and hatred! Does the corniness go any further?'

'Not further. Just in-between. Because between love and hatred lie the gradated pit-stops of affection, cordiality, mere tolerance, apathy, resentment and detestation.

'The sad part is that even though we're free to choose our habitat zone from the love-hate spectrum, we rarely exercise that choice. Instead, we keep wallowing in a narrow band that's been relegated to us by some strange quirk of fate. And *that* is the reason why—save for an extreme interference by providence—people tend to remain about as happy, or as sad, as they always were. As happy or sad as they've decided to be.'

'And what has all this got to do with first love?' demanded Raghu.

'First love,' answered Abeer, 'is one such interference by providence. It's the time in life when your relegated zone becomes dysfunctional, and you are—if only temporarily—transported to a zone of pure and potent love. In fact, according to Maupassant, you at that time aren't so much in love with a person as you're in love with love. So that's a time when all hatred is flushed out, a time when your tolerance levels increase, a time when nobody seems despicable. And as a result of all of that, you become moronically happy.'

Raghu considered as Abeer continued.

'You're right. It's corny. But "corny" is usually the crust of repetitiousness that covers a truth. So you see, it's true too. Sustained happiness is possible only by draining the heart of even the mildest form of hatred. And it is to acquaint us with this fact that nature has programmed the phenomenon of first love. Just imagine, if love for one can result in that kind of happiness, what kind of happiness would a love for all yield! And mind you, I'm not invoking religion and the world beyond at all. I'm talking of happiness *here and now.*'

The phrase rang a bell. Raghu was reminded of the 'here and now' couple who'd suddenly found themselves without an engine. There was perhaps an answer for them here.

'But why do you mention religion in this overtly defensive tone? A person like you!' Having gone through the uneasy bout featuring Lila, Raghu was keen to get his own back.

'Not in the least,' answered Abeer matter of factly, 'I mention religion because a large part of it deals with what we're discussing. Religion talks of sin and virtue, which are supposed to be parallels for misery and happiness. Apparently, they're also parallels for hatred and love.'

'Come again?'

'Hatred is the equivalent of sin. Sin is the equivalent of misery. So hatred gone implies misery gone. And once misery is gone, happiness fills in the void!'

'But I still don't see the connection.'

'What connection?'

'Sins and hatred.'

'But isn't it obvious? Take any of the seven cardinal sins from Christianity: Greed, Gluttony, Sloth, Wrath, Envy, Pride, Lust. One good look at them and you realize that hatred lies at the root of all. Pride says I'm superior, and hence by default, you're inferior. Greed functions on depriving a fellow being. Wrath is resentment personified. Gluttony and sloth are self hatred. And Envy obviously is the most common and most naked form of hatred. Hatred, all! Hatred in its myriad incarnations! So you see, it's not without reason that learned men across religions have been telling us to rid ourselves of sins. The lapse has been in our comprehension. When we hear them talking about the benefits of a sinless life, we impulsively assume that they're referring to an afterworld; whereas the benefits are very much for the here and now.'

'Then your learned men ought to specify that point. They should know that takers for the afterlife are decreasing by the day.'

'And is that the way you feel too?' asked Abeer.

'I don't know whether I believe in an afterlife or not. I just don't obsess over it because I don't find it too relevant. I mean, all that I call *me* has a lot to do with my personality. And a lot of my personality is lodged in my memory. And if I'm not carrying my memory—the surface part, not your deep seated *samskaras*—into the next life, there *is* no me. Then why should I be concerned with what happens to my reincarnation?'

The slight hint of incomprehension in Abeer's aspect prompted Raghu to elaborate, 'Okay, let's take it this way. Imagine a scenario where you intend to seek revenge from a man who'd once wronged you. And imagine that after years and years of waiting, such a chance does finally come your way. But then, just as you're about to serve it out to him, cold, you realize that your to-be victim is suffering from Alzheimer's. His memory's gone. He absolutely fails to recognize you. Now, would you still go ahead with your revenge? I think not. Because for all practical purposes, the man who had wronged you is already dead.

'And if a man can die while he's alive, he certainly *can* die when he's dead.'

'Interesting,' smiled Abeer.

Raghu, made uneasy by the compliment, hastened to fill the silence. 'But I guess afterlife does have its uses. As carrot and stick it both scares and entices people into good behaviour. Besides, it's a wonderful tool to explain away what existentialists call absurdism. Anything bad happens to a good man and you can conveniently cast it off as bad karma from a previous life.'

'Wow! The devout Hindu has come a long way.'

'Not long enough though. Because from an afterlife of souls, the devout Hindu has merely shifted his belief to an afterlife of electromagnetic waves.'

Abeer wrinkled his brow and, with a slight nod of the head, gestured to Raghu to go on.

'It's a vague notion,' hesitated Raghu, 'It's a theory about emotions. Especially, strong emotions.'

'What about them?'

'I feel that emotions are something special. They aren't just data stored in the brain that'll be erased once the hydrocarbon-energy supply is switched off. I'm kind of convinced that emotions have a parallel existence outside of our craniums; that there's another medium where they subsist, where they linger. Somewhat like invisible electromagnetic waves.

'A lot many things point in that direction you see. Take for example the soothing aura of holy places. Is that aura not better explained by the devout emotions of the frequenting millions? Or consider telepathy.'

'C'mon! Telepathy is hardly a proven phenomenon.'

'Who said we're discussing proven phenomenon? I'm simply attempting a hypothetical explanation to popular myths. So, as I was saying, we have telepathy and we have the folklore surrounding blessings and curses. *Dua* and *bud-dua*. Isn't that strong emotions travelling from the corporeal world to the ethereal medium, and then from the ethereal world back to the corporeal? And ghosts! Purportedly, ghosts are people with unfulfilled wishes who died untimely deaths. *Wishes* is the catchword here. Also, doesn't religion tell us that good deeds will get us heaven; but to attain emancipation, we need to rid ourselves of desire. Desire! Emotion again. Or take the mystic aura that surrounds snakes,' went on Raghu undeterred. 'Their connect with Shiva and the wish-fulfilling *mani*. If there indeed is an ethereal medium for strong emotions, it surely would be most accessible to a limbless creature that has limited means to execute its will; a creature whose unfulfilled desires are likely to fester into an intense concoction. And,' said Raghu taking a dramatic pause, 'isn't it possible that that ethereal medium is the reason why men of religion are asked to be sexually abstemious? The sexual urge, after all, is a very strong emotion. If you can manage to bottle it up, it could perhaps serve as a sort of carrier wave to that elusive medium.'

Abeer gave a slight nod that could well have been agreement. Raghu, who was suddenly more than a little embarrassed, hastened to take the attention away from himself. 'You were telling me about happiness here and now.'

'Oh yes,' replied Abeer, at once getting the drift behind Raghu's last remark. 'Here and now! That's the catchphrase. Because happiness has to flow to you *here* and *now*. And it has to flow to you as a natural consequence of certain actions, not as a bequest from some vindictive book-keeping deity.'

This was new to Raghu. He sought to confirm he'd heard it right. 'When you call happiness a natural consequence of certain actions, do you imply it to be inevitable?'

'Inevitable *and* imminent,' was the reply.

'But isn't that going too far? Do you really think something as evanescent and elusive as happiness can be made to follow orders?'

'Well save for a few dissidents, people *do* agree that almost everything in this universe follows an order. Even disorder, which you call entropy, seems to be orchestrated according to an order, a set of rules. And if there is a set of rules for the universe—

this marvel in heavy engineering—I'm sure there also has to be a set of rules for the well being of those who inhabit it. Also, I'm pretty sure that learned men and seers—over a period of time—must have got an insight into that set of rules.'

'Then what prevented them from sharing that knowledge?'

'Inadequate communication tools,' answered Abeer, 'because how do you explain *red* to a blind person? Similarly, how do you explain something that lies beyond the five senses to somebody who uses just five? And I'm not talking about inadequacy of range. I'm not talking ultrasound or infrared. I'm talking about a whole new sensory perception. Because mind you, to think that the world has just five sensations to offer would be akin to behaving like a congregation of snakes which decides that there is no such thing as sound.'

'That's an interesting view,' conceded Raghu.

'But perception apart, there must have been another hurdle to communication,' went on Abeer. 'That of the intellectual divide between the seers and their audience. It's this divide which must've thwarted even the existing tools of communication from being used to full effect. And the seers would've been left with no option but to try and explain things in a more comprehensible manner. But since comprehension is not independent of context—a thought duly echoed by the great Ludwig Wittgenstein—a seer's method of explanation must obviously have depended upon the culture of the people he was addressing. It also would've depended upon the period in history that those people occupied. Understandable then that the various religions, with their origins separated in time and space, are cosmetically different from each other. But peel through the surface and the core comes out to be the same. The purpose, the same. Religion intends you to lead a happy life.'

'Doesn't seem so from the face of it. Not at least from the various restrictions it seeks to impose,' put in Raghu.

'Several of those restrictions are nothing but vested interests. Of course, some are valid as well.'

'Like the cardinal sins!'

'Like the cardinal sins. And our mistake in tackling cardinal sins is that we do it by dint of willpower alone.'

'Is there another way?' asked Raghu, who had almost prepared himself for a lecture on self control and restraint.

'Well there's no standard formula but it does help if you attack sin from a previously untried angle. For example, you could try personalized logic.'

Raghu shot an inquisitive glance. Abeer obliged.

'Okay, let me get to examples,' he said. 'Let's begin with the sin that's the most common of all: Wrath. Now here's an ailment that cannot be taken lightly because it assails both your emotional and physical well being. Surprisingly—for a majority of people—there are just two lines of treatment available. You can either vent your anger or you can temporarily suppress it. Needless to say, none of these treatments are adequate. The former is detrimental to your relationships and bank accounts. And the latter is like planting a seed that'll sprout into a happiness-killing cancer.

'Given the consequences, you'd think that nobody in his sane mind would want to carry this baggage of suppressed anger. But the surprising part is that almost everyone does. How? Well, because in order to carry the seed of anger, you don't actually need to harbour an urge to get even with your tormentor. Your merely wanting to see him put into place, or your simple wish to *show* it to him, suffices. In fact, you can be said to be carrying anger if so much as the recollection of an incident or person perturbs you.

'Now, while I don't recommend flying off the handle in every argument, I would say that that's preferable to anger of the suppressed kind. That's preferable because the damage caused by it is less permanent and less grave.'

Raghu lit up a cigarette before he ventured, 'But "carrying" anger is an involuntary phenomenon. What can you possibly do about it?'

'First and foremost,' replied Abeer, 'it would be good to acknowledge that anger cannot be fought . Eventually, you'll lose. The only way you can outwit anger is by transcending it. And one way to approach that is to view anger as a third person; to *observe* it whenever it strikes. Observe it taking command of your faculties. Observe the way it fastens your pulse, raises your temperature, poisons your brain. Observe how it first reaches for the jugular—reaches for those tender emotions and complexes where it knows you're most vulnerable. Observe, simply observe. The more detachedly you observe, the more easily you can prevent it from taking over. Remember, anger is not an armed robber; it's a thief. If it enters your house and realizes that it's under observation, it'll go back empty handed. And more the number of such empty-handed visits, lesser the number of future attempts to be expected from the intruder.'

'And what if this formula—watching over anger as one watches over a thief—doesn't work?'

'Two solutions. Solution number one is to reduce the load. During the phase when you're still training to keep anger at bay, proactively keep away from situations that induce it.'

'And solution two?'

'Solution two is an engineering trick. When the formula you're using seems to have a snag, revert to first principles. Strike at the root of the sin itself. Strike at the hatred. Develop compassion. Get into the shoes of the one who is angering you. Remember, in nine cases out of ten, people do not intend to anger you deliberately. They act that way because that is the way they are. That is their normal mode of function. Life did not afford them the perspective and privileges that it did to you. Now surely that calls for understanding, not self-harming anger. You don't break your own leg when you encounter someone with a foot deformity!'

A meeting at the Student Activity Centre had ended and left the road clogged with scores of students. Abeer and Raghu waited in silence for the crowd to disburse. While they were doing so, hints of a pensive smile gradually made its way to the corners of Abeer's lips. He had been reminded of something.

'You've been to my parents' place. Do you remember the corner near my house where daily-wage labourers used to gather?'

'Yes I do,' answered Raghu, 'I do because we had an incident with those guys in my very first visit.'

'Incidents with those guys happened almost every day. That in fact is the reason I brought up their example. But tell me, which incident do *you* refer to?'

'There was this good-for-nothing lout who stood in the middle of the road and wouldn't budge . When he finally moved, it was of his own sweet will; and to make us realize that it actually *is* his sweet will, he duly smirked at us. Your dad had smiled back.'

'What else could dad have done?' smiled Abeer, 'Now this is where the first principles thing comes in. Compassion! Let's with compassion peep into the life of the person whom you call a good-for-nothing lout.

'This lout, Raghu, relies on gross physical labour to feed himself and his family. Day in and day out. And all that a day's work affords him is a hundred and fifty rupees; an amount that doesn't buy you a bottle of beer in a decent restaurant. Yes, the lout also has a foul mouth, a taste of which you'd have got had you ventured to start an argument with him. But do you know where that came from? Right! Listening to verbal abuses is an integral part of his job profile. Come to think of it, it's difficult to imagine an entity that ever treated our lout with respect. No, not even his wife; they thankfully have very strong women's lib in his society. And yet, never having been treated with respect is not the worst that our lout has suffered. The worst is that he lives a life that's bereft of hope.

'Do you know why people like you and me are able to swallow an unpalatable present? Mainly because the future appears to proffer a nebulous hope; because beneath the translucent layer of our apprehensions, lies the half-visible assurance that all will be well in the end. But for the lout, it's all pitch dark beneath that translucent layer. He *knows* that his life is a series of a hundred and fifty rupee days strung together. And only till his ill-fed health holds out.

'So when such a lout stands in front of my car and derives satisfaction at being one-up on society, am I to deny him that fleeting pleasure?'

A silence followed.

'Moving on to the next sin,' spoke Abeer abruptly, 'we arrive at Envy. Now who's it that we're most envious of?'

'Whom?' asked Raghu, not wanting to hazard a guess.

'Those close to us, those whom we know well. We're never envious of Roger Federer or Bill Gates. Not at any rate one-tenth as envious as we are of an affluent neighbour or relative. And why? Because the neighbor and the relative tread on the same planet as us. Roger Federer and Bill Gates are from Mars—though we do try to pull them down to earth at every opportunity.

I mean, what else does the heavy sale of tabloids and gossip magazines prove?

'But enough about the passing envy that we hold for M/s Federer & Co. The point is that when it comes to real hardcore envy, we can't seem to look much beyond our relatives, friends, colleagues and neighbors—people like us. And because they are people like us, we feel that the fortune which befalls them could very easily have befallen us. Hence the envy! So Envy, you see, is nothing but the first manifest symptom of a disease called cognitive shortsightedness. And therefore, the easiest way to treat it is to get vision-aid that helps you look beyond. We need to genuinely believe that Roger Federer and Bill Gates are people like us. What they are capable of, we are too. As this belief begins to sink in, our vision involuntarily undergoes a quantum change. The constricted view is replaced by a world-engulfing panoramic one. Now since the human brain cannot handle being envious of the entire world, it automatically transforms envy into inspiration.'

'You know,' said Raghu with a slight shake of the head, 'no matter what I do for my short-sightedness, I'll always envy you for your uncomplicated way of looking at things.'

'I'll have to debar that compliment on precautionary grounds. Pride is what I was coming to next,' answered Abeer

Raghu smiled, primarily out of politeness.

'Please, no half-hearted smiles. What we need is full-throttled laughter. Pride calls for it. God! It amazes me to see the stuff people find conceit in. Why, even their diseases. The immaculate detail in which they describe their symptoms; and the way they take offence when you mention an acquaintance who suffered similarly!'

'Offended by the acquaintance?'

'Yup. He takes away exclusivity you see, thereby forcing them on a hunt for another unique symptom.'

Raghu laughed.

'But seriously,' continued Abeer after a pause. 'How much pride can there be in winning a lottery? Because come to think of it, even the best of us are just that. A lucky draw from the gene pool. All right, make that a lucky draw coupled with a few coincidences—what neighbours we had, which school our parents took a fancy to, who sat next to us in class, which book we read at what stage of our life, and some such. In fact, even our infatuations are a matter of proximity and coincidence, as is perhaps our entire personality.

'Then how, I ask, can any intelligent person court pride?'

'Well I for one can't,' answered Raghu, tongue firmly in cheek.

'Your paradox comes in good time. I was finally coming to that. Contradiction. You see, all these sin-killing personal logics and techniques are good to get you started. But once underway, you'll have to come back to the basic principle—love and compassion.'

'Is that a must? I mean, why can't reason carry us all the way?'

'Because reason has its limitations. Our understanding has its limitations.'

Raghu's expression indicated that he didn't quite see what kind of limitations were being talked about, and Abeer had to elaborate, 'Take the example of bonobos and chimpanzees. They share 98 per cent of their DNA with us, and they're known to perform some physical and mental tasks that can be said to be fairly complex. But on this basis, can we extrapolate that somewhere in the future chimpanzees will be able to comprehend quantum theory?'

'Of course not.'

'Then isn't it vain to assume that a 2 per cent DNA jump results in a limitless increase in intelligence; that it enables us to comprehend all that there is to be comprehended in the universe? Mind you, I'm not talking about undiscovered software. I'm talking about hardware limitations.'

'Okay! So because there are limitations to our understanding, we seek refuge in love and compassion.' The sarcasm in his tone was a knee-jerk reaction to the unintended put-down.

'Yes. Because in love and compassion lies the answer to Aari's engine. In love and compassion lies the answer to why Abhay isn't happy despite being both righteous and successful.'

Raghu was suddenly all ears. When he had referred these questions to Abeer the previous evening, the reply they had elicited was a cursory one.

'Ordinary happiness,' commenced Abeer 'is never a state. It's always, *always* a transition from a lower plane to a higher one. And therein lies the answer to your two paradoxes.

'What Aari has done till now is climb one hill after another. But with every up, there has also been a down. Besides, the whole thing has been quite repetitive. No wonder Aari's all bored and exhausted by now. Abhay, on the other hand, has been scaling a mountain. With him the scenario has been all up and up; and it was only when he was tripped-up by certain circumstances that a problem arose. Not only did that fall deliver him a rude shock, it also apprised him of how close to the mountain peak he was. And unfortunately, instead of buoying him up, that chance sighting overwhelmed our climber with a feeling of futility. It saddened him with the realization that there was nowhere left to go.'

'So you're telling me they're both doomed?'

'We're all doomed! We're doomed as long as our happiness stays tethered to this Cartesian plane of coordinates. The escape, as I said, lies in love and compassion. That's what propels you into a coordinate-less space-time continuum of bliss.'

'And your so-called sin-killing techniques? What of them?'

'Well in most cases they're no more than the training tyres of a bicycle. Though you're expected to get rid of them once their job's done, it really doesn't matter if you don't. All they cause is a slight inconvenience. However, in certain cases these techniques can be like the booster engines of a multi-stage rocket. They need to be jettisoned in time in order to achieve appropriate velocity.'

'And what according to you is impeding Abhay's flight?'

'His pride. I thought that was obvious. Then again, it's perhaps not all that obvious, because his is not the kind of pride you encounter in everyday life. His is a pride that's interlocked with his virtues. The stronger they get, the more they enhance it. Now we all know that Abhay never lies. But do you know why? Well because when you lie to someone, you temporarily elevate that person to your own status, if not higher. And Abhay doesn't bequeath that kind of respect very easily.'

Raghu laughed aloud.

'Wait till you hear how he got the better of his anger,' Abeer continued.

'All ears.'

'It's an incident from the years when things were just beginning to look up for him. This particular day I talk of, he was in a rather prickly mood. It took just a slight instigation from one of his small-time suppliers to set him off. But even as the supplier was being supplied with a piece of Abhay's mind, the phone rang. There was this very important customer on the line. The customer, Abhay tells me, was trying to rekindle to his advantage a matter that had been emphatically settled a few days ago. Now, keeping in mind the mood Abhay was in, guess what his response was?'

Raghu prompted Abeer to go on.

'Abhay politely explained the whole situation to the important customer once more, never once losing his cool.'

'Uh-huh?'

'Then one full day after the episode, it dawned upon him. He realized how wonderfully wise his temper was. A temper that knew exactly when to roar and when to purr.'

'And then?'

'And then Abhay made a sort of commitment to himself—that he would never express anger at a person upon whom he *can*. Unluckily for him, the number of such people has been increasing ever since. I think he's actually lost his urge to shout at people now.'

Abeer looked towards Raghu expectantly. He had lucidly made his point and was anticipating a reaction. But when none was forthcoming, he finally remarked, 'Do you still not see the limitations of these techniques? Abhay could give up lies and anger, but only at the cost of enhanced pride. It's like using stitches to seal a wound and then not bothering to remove them later.'

'What if your stitches are the harmless type, the self-dissolving ones?'

'Well good for you if that is the case. As the great Spinoza says, "and in the end there's just one virtue—intelligence." So if you're able to dissolve away the stitches because of your acumen to perceive the big-picture—the acumen to see your passions for the "inadequate ideas" that they are—there's nothing to prevent you from walking the path of happiness. But still, I think that the method of love and compassion is the easiest of them all. Love, after all, *is* our natural state. The only reason it putrefies is that it lacks an outlet. Provide the outlet and love begins to flow; happiness begins to flow. Think about it, what is first love but an outlet. What are kids? Outlets again. Why, even pets are outlets. I mean, how else do you account for people burying their faces in unwashed masses of fur?'

Raghu chuckled. He knew that Abeer, an avid animal lover, had said that to rag him on his phobia of dogs.

'You might want to try this little experiment,' said Abeer after a short pause. He had spoken in a seemingly casual tone, and Raghu at once knew that what was to follow was something Abeer considered important.

'Any given Sunday,' began Abeer, 'when your mood is amiable and little is playing on the mind, play some good light music on the audio system. Then settle yourself on your favourite couch with a steaming cup of coffee. Or beer, if that's what you prefer. Now close your eyes and start thinking of all the people you like. The ultimate aim of course is to think that you *like* all people. But since we can't get there in one single step, we'll start with small ones. We'll start with the most obvious candidate—your daughter. Just close your eyes and think of her. Think about the most loving moments you've spent with her. Think about the loving lisp with which she says "papa". Think about the way she kisses you good night every evening. Think about that time in the fair when you thought she was lost. How frantically she'd hugged you when you'd finally found her, and how your mutual tears were impossible to tell apart. Think about her vulnerability. What if her best friend in school broke her little heart? Think about all the love you'd need to give her in such a situation. Think about it in earnest, and you'll sense that same love gradually dripping into the cauldron of your heart.

'And as this cauldron fills up, you will feel a certain mellowness set in. Take a sip and move on to another kin or close friend. Mind you, this exercise is not about analyzing people in depth. Not at this stage. All you're supposed to do right now is to project a character on the screen of your mind and think up of reasons to love that character. Think up of all the fine qualities you can attribute to it. And when you run out of fine reasons and fine qualities, promptly move on to the next kin.

'When you appreciate all those small and not-so-small sacrifices that your wife has made for you, when you remember the way your parents' face lights up each time they meet you, when you think of the night your friend stayed awake with you in the hospital; the dripping fastens. The cauldron is now about half full and on a slow simmer. Time to throw in the condiments: people you interact little with, people you're on so-so terms with. That office boy, for example. Nice chap, isn't he? While in office, always running from one end to the other. While at home, not able to make them meet. A reasonably fine job he delivers under the circumstances—or in any case, a reasonably fine effort. Also, once you're able to do away with the belief about him being on earth for the sole purpose of serving you, you at once become a tad more appreciative of those efforts. Yes, the office boy is okay. As is your aunt from Kolkata! Agreed that the jumpers she brings for you are outright rotten. But her taste-buds are not her fault, are they? Besides, at least she tries. When was the last time *you* bought her a present?

'Its final then, the aunt from Kolkata is definitely nice. So is the secretary at your friend's office. And so is the *paanwala* at the street corner who so obsequiously sells cigarette packets to you. The guard in your housing society; that chap with the amiable smile whom you often run into at the club; nice people all.'

Abeer paused. They had reached the campus boundary. Raghu wanted to turn back. Abeer pointed at the small desolate gate that led beyond. Tentatively, they took it.

'By now,' continued Abeer, 'your coffee mug would be near empty, and your cauldron about full. The full cauldron would be pulsating with a half-cooked happiness. Bask in the warmth of this compassion. Savour the rising aroma as you prepare to add the main ingredient to the dish—the ingredient that is unpalatable in its raw. Yes, I refer to people you abhor, people you don't see eye to eye with. Be it the adversary from office, that big snob of a neighbour, or the boss from your last job whom you never really forgave for that public dressing down; it's time to cook their goose!

'Consider these people. Think about them not as characters but as human beings who are liable to falter. Think about them in their homes amidst their families, their fears, their insecurities. Yes, your boss does have a family he goes back to each evening. And since he does have a family, he too—like everybody else— isn't immune from occasionally bringing his personal problems to work. If under their influence he gives you an uncalled for reprimand, don't take it to heart. Just like the office boy didn't when *you* yelled at him. Besides, I'm sure there must have been times when your boss showed himself in *some* positive light. Play and replay that little clip in your mind. You'll realize that the compassion brewing in the cauldron will slowly tenderize all the little chunks of hatred. Also, as each such chunk dissolves, it will release a joy that will run like a spasm through your entire being.

'And for those chunks that were only partly tenderized, well, there's always the next Sunday.'

Raghu was reminded of his recent visit to Kalra's house.

The main door to the residence had been ajar and when no one responded to the bell, Raghu had entered unannounced. He found Kalra in the backyard. Dressed in droopy Bermudas and flanked by his two kids, Kalra was holding a sloppy sandwich in one hand and a decrepit table-tennis racquet in the other. It was a sight that instantly metamorphosed—if only temporarily—the conniving yes-man into a vulnerable family guy.

The emotions Raghu had then experienced now began to fall in context. He parted his lips to say something but then checked himself. 'Go on,' prompted Abeer. Never one to concede a point easily, Raghu began with some reluctance, 'The fact, Abeer, is that I live in a real world. Then why this experiment with unreal parameters and strange test conditions? Why not analyze people for real rather than concentrate on just their positive aspects?'

'Because there's nothing to be gained by concentrating on the negative. The rancor and resentment that you carry for people is harming *you*, not them. And when you decide to overlook or forgive people's wrongs, it's yourself you're doing the biggest favour to.

'Think of it, your happiest days are those when everybody—or almost everybody—seems nice. True likewise, is also the opposite.'

'But c'mon, isn't it a bit over the top—all of a sudden getting into goody-goody mode with all and sundry?'

'Who says you have to do it suddenly? Know this. If you at all intend to make it last, go about that whole process very gradually. In the spectrum which features love, affection, cordiality, tolerance, apathy, resentment and detestation; move *one* notch at a time. Try to love those whom you are affectionate towards, and be affectionate to those whom you are cordial to. And should you find it difficult to promote someone from detestation to resentment, just let it be for the time being. You can consider them in round two when you're about to advance everyone else by another notch.'

'And is that going to be any easier?'

'Why yes. For here too, like in your other pursuits, you get better with practice. Mind, I said *you*. Because at no point are you to expect any change from the people you're reviewing. The change has to be in *your* perception of them. Remember, happiness happens when love is allowed an outlet to flow; and an outlet happens when your love finds worthy receptacles for itself. What we're doing here is creating those worthy receptacles.'

There was a prolonged silence. Raghu realized that there was some sense in what Abeer was saying. Just listening to it had made him feel somewhat elated. But of course, there was no way he was going to make an explicit confession of that. No matter how poignant the scene, guys never like to be caught with damp eyes at the movies.

'Lust,' said Raghu at last, 'you didn't talk about the sin called Lust.'

'That's because lust isn't as thinly veiled an incarnation of hatred as the other sins. It asks for one's own pleasure, not for the pain of another.'

'Unless we are talking sado-masochism,' smiled Raghu.

'Unless we are talking sado-masochism,' repeated Abeer with a laugh. It was some time before he continued, 'It may not be a direct incarnation, but Lust nevertheless has its ways of getting at you. The web that it weaves is intricate. It starts off by portraying itself as something natural and basic. And once it has established that reputation, and has seamlessly blended into the scheme of things, it gradually begins to spiral out of control. It then commences to feed off its own success and grows insatiable with each victory; thereby making it the most difficult of the sins to give up. You see, it's not for nothing that we call lust the original sin.'

'But what you're pointing out are the reasons for it being hard to overcome. The question is, *why* is it a sin?'

'For the same reason as the others; because it is an impediment to your happiness. It tampers with the supply lines of love and affection to your fellow beings. Once it has spiraled out of control, it makes you view the object of your lust as exactly that—an object. Not a human being in its entirety but an object of specific utility. As Pope John Paul II pointed out, the problem with pornography is not that it shows too much of the person. The problem is that it shows far too little. And you see, once you start viewing people as objects, it's only natural that covetousness, greed, jealousy, and even pride, get into the picture. Add powerful hormones like oxytocin to that mix, and you eventually land up in an endless alley of blind obsession.'

'You can hardly call it endless. There *is* such a thing as gratification.'

'Is there? Because a lot of people believe that lust subsists on ever-changing variety. Of course, I speak only from hearsay.'

Raghu laughed. He had been reminded of Aari—the person who didn't need to rely on hearsay to reach that very same conclusion. He was glad he had steered the conversation in this realm. Here lay the queries which he wanted answered. 'And what according to you,' he finally asked, smearing his question with nonchalance, 'is the way out of this alley of frustration? Can lust really be tackled? Or should we simply get working on a patent for Argaiv?'

'What's Argaiv?'

'The reverse of Viagra.'

'No I don't think Argaiv would be a good idea,' replied Abeer matter-of-factly. 'Lust is a natural instinct. If we left it to play itself out naturally, I'm pretty sure it wouldn't cause much harm. Animals never overfeed; and even at the peak of their mating season, never fornicate more than their species requires them to.'

'Then why do humans?'

'Because we allow intellect to interfere with the instincts. Somewhere along the line, we've allowed the balance between intellect and instinct to be irreparably disturbed. The scales have now tilted sharply in favour of intellect. Uninfluenced instinct is an oxymoron. It's a relic of a bygone era. No, instincts are no longer capable of playing it out naturally. People are instigated to crave more than what is necessary, eat more than what their hunger dictates, and fornicate more than they would have if they were uncultured cavemen or bonobos.'

'Okay, so you're telling me that lust within bounds isn't a sin any more than a healthy diet isn't gluttony.'

'Quite. And I think the parallel you draw may hold an answer to your question about tackling lust. You see, if a man has been consciously availing the benefits of a healthy diet for years together, it's unlikely that he'll give in to unwholesome food or overeating. I guess the same thing applies to a man who's lived in conscious harmony with a lust that isn't inappropriate. Mind you, the keyword here is *conscious*.'

Raghu allowed some time for the thought to sink in. Yet Abeer went on, 'But yes, lust *is* complicated; will take more than such simple parallels to decipher. I think we should save lust for another day.'

'But haven't you done that for long enough already? You're over thirty-five,' joked Raghu. Then buoyed by Abeer's smile, went on to add, 'It's one thing being sublime, but quite another to sublimate from adolescence to middle age; and give youth a miss altogether.'

'It takes all kinds to make a world,' put in Abeer.

'Perhaps it does,' replied Raghu. He was quick to perceive the modest Abeer's unease. He deflected the conversation. 'I think we better make a move if we are to catch up with Abhay. As it is, most of tomorrow will be taken up by work.'

Abeer nodded in affirmation.

'Must be an awesome feeling,' went on Raghu, 'Raising an empire from dust, and then bequeathing it all for a cause. All in one lifetime!'

Hardly had he finished saying that when his cell phone rang. It was Nandini calling. Incidentally, the first word she uttered was 'Abhay', and Raghu, without even hearing what she had to say further, took the instrument slightly away from his ear and pointing to it quipped to Abeer, 'Talk of Da-Will and the devil is here!' Then laughing at his own wisecrack, he eventually got back to hear what Nandini had to say.

All colour soon drained from his face. Abhay had had an accident.

Doors of perception

Raghu was frantically saying something to the hospital receptionist when someone touched him on the shoulder. He turned around to find that it was Nandini. 'He's in the ICU,' she whispered, 'severe head injury.'

'Which way?' he demanded impatiently.

'But they won't allow you in,' she cautioned, even as she led the way.

Nandini was right. The staff at the ICU gate didn't allow any of them in; though one attendant did relent to take in a message to Tania. It took five long minutes for Tania to show up. She appeared surprisingly composed and to the tacit question on Raghu's face, replied 'All tests have been run. They say it's going to be a major operation.'

A long silence ensued; a shared and exclusive silence, islands of which can often be found in bustling hospital corridors.

Abeer was the first to speak. 'It's late. I think you should get home to Vini,' he said to Raghu.

Nandini answered before Raghu could, 'I've arranged for Menaaz to take care of Vini.' It was her adamant tone and Raghu knew there was no point arguing.

In about an hour it was time for Abhay's operation. The hospital attendants wheeled him away into what is sadistically referred to as a theater. Its gates swung open and closed and Tania was left behind helplessly staring at them. There was nothing she could do but wait for the proclamation that would come once they reopened. As she stood looking at those gates, she was suddenly inundated with memories of the time spent with Abhay. They weren't pleasant memories; at least not in their undoctored state. She struggled to keep them away but in vain. The more she pushed them out, the greater the vehemence with which they returned. Finally, she gave up and let them be.

It took a good four hours for the operation. 'The procedures were successful,' informed the surgeon, 'but being a head injury, a definite prognosis can only be made once he regains consciousness.'

'When can we expect that?' asked Tania.

The doctor shrugged his shoulders in reply. His benign expression ensured that the shrug wasn't taken for apathy; and that it remained a categorical 'I don't know'. As he mildly patted Tania's back to comfort her, he slipped in some advice alongside 'The anesthesia will take time to wear off. I suggest you get some rest in the while.' The counsel was given not because it was expected to be followed but merely out of a sense of duty and convention. Tania, predictably, did not heed it. She walked away towards the ICU where Abhay was to be brought. 'We'll be downstairs in the lobby,' said Nandini, understanding Tania's need to be by herself.

Once they were settled in the lobby, Nandini started to narrate in detail what she had till now conveyed in bits and pieces; about how a kid had suddenly run across the road, how Abhay had braked and swerved, and how a car coming from behind had hit him on the side—his side. Luckily, one of the people in the vicinity turned out to be a former employee. He had rushed Abhay to hospital and informed Abhay's office of the incident. Then since the office-staff wasn't able to contact Abhay's parents, they got in touch with Tania instead. Nandini was with Tania when she received that call.

Nandini kept going with her narrative but Raghu wasn't really listening. He was merely watching her lips move and letting the sound of her words soothe his frayed nerves into sanity. To him, her presence was all that mattered. The veil of mortality which the accident had brought between them had faithfully stripped all sights and sounds of everything that was extraneous. 'Try and get some sleep,' he said at last, as he gently rested her head on his shoulder.

The long night trudged away at a snail's pace and dawn turned out to be nothing but a bleak grey inception. Abhay woke up to a vegetative condition. He could neither move nor speak. And in the months that followed, those solemn eyes became his sole means of communication with the outside world.

Or almost...

'At first, mixed tints of bitterness was all that those eyes conveyed,' Raghu was telling a young college-going Vini. His club was hosting a tournament for veterans and the two of them were awaiting his turn at the sidelines of the squash courts. 'But Tania surprised all of us with the way she looked after him. I've no clue how she managed that tightrope walk because we found him neither disgruntled from lack of care, nor grumpy from too much of it. Also, out of all of us, *she* was the one who could best read those eyes—as plainly as if she were reading a book.

'It wasn't long before he was *discussing* the school project with Abeer. We were happy that there was something to keep him occupied. In fact, I got worried about what would happen once the project got on track and started to run on its own steam. I even urged Abeer to feign some roadblocks to prolong Abhay's involvement. But we never got around to that. Abhay backed away from the project ahead of time. I'd forgotten that he was the architect of many business ventures, and that he would foresee before any of us that critical juncture from where things roll on their own.

'And then something strange happened. Instead of the despondent ennui that we'd all feared he'll fall into, Abhay entered into an epoch of easy bliss. There was no way to account for it, and the only explanation seems to be the one which Abeer propounds—that being handicapped is what it took to free him of his "I". Of course, things could have gone the other way too, says Abeer. That same handicap could have made him even more entrenched in the "I". But given the spiritual footing where Abhay was positioned, what in fact happened was the more likely outcome of the two.

'I'm told he actually smiled when he passed on.'

The silence which followed was dotted with the intermittent calling-out of participant names. It was Vini who spoke first. 'Mama says you didn't meet him much after the accident.'

'No I didn't. For obvious reasons.'

The twenty-year-old didn't see what was obvious about the reasons. She wanted to ask him that but was interrupted from doing so. The call for his match had come up.

It turned out to be a closely fought contest. Raghu's opponent discovered early in the play that Raghu's key weapon was his backhand volley. He quickly got around to offsetting it with the use of high balls, clinging balls and the occasional low ball. The clinging balls forced some opportunities and the opponent was prompt in putting them away. Raghu lost the first game. Then the short break which preceded the second one allowed him occasion to rethink his tactics. He began by controlling the pace of the rally and moving his opponent around with his boast. Importantly, he also took some risks by imposing his volley. The strategy paid off and the match score stood evened.

By the time they got to the middle of the final game, both players had exhausted all elements of surprise that each could spring on the other. The outcome of the match now hinged—like does the outcome of every critical endeavour—upon how well one blended the prosaic basics with risky scintillation.

Ultimately, Raghu lost. After the lob in response to his drop-shot had died in the nick of the back wall, he genially shook hands with the winner, thanked the referee, and walked off towards Vini at the sidelines. He made a mock sad face at her and sank into his chair with an air of pretended despair. 'You look unusually relaxed for a loser,' she teased.

'But that's the way I usually am,' he replied calmly; then after a pause, added, 'Perhaps more so today.'

'Because today I brought up Abhay Uncle?' she posed.

'Not just that,' he hesitated. 'I guess talking about Abhay reminded me of another good friend—a friend and his stalled engines.'

'Stalled engines! Care to elaborate?'

'Uhhh…I think we'll let that wait,' said Raghu with a smile.

The self-consciousness which had accompanied that smile was telling, and Vini persisted 'Don't be a prude, dad.'

'Okay,' he yielded after some thought 'I think stalled engines can be approached from another angle. Nietzsche's! Are you aware of the funda of Nietzsche's twins?' She shook her head and he continued, 'Nietzsche says that a person's happiness and sadness are monozygotic twins. They have to be the same size. So, when you're incited to great happiness by an attainment, you automatically make yourself vulnerable to an equally great misery—the misery which would come with the loss, or the fear of loss, or simply a wearing off, of that attainment. Conversely, when you inure yourself to the pain that arises from losing something, you also inure yourself to the pleasure that lay in relishing it. You thus deprive yourself of things to look forward to, things that keep you going. You extinguish with full cognition the very force that propels you.

'And that extinguished force, young girl, is a stalled engine.'

'You *can* be depressing when you want to.'

Raghu shrugged his shoulders in reply as he started to pack his stuff into the carry-bag. Vini waited. She was hoping he would say something reassuring. But when he didn't, she finally blurted out, 'Okay! So what's the way out?'

'The way out is what you just witnessed.'

Her blank look, which was accompanied by a slight shake of the head, urged him to explicate. He relented. 'You saw me lose a match, and you saw that it didn't affect me. Therefore, according to Nietzsche's theory of monozygotic twins, winning shouldn't have mattered to me either. But you know it very well that that's not true. You clearly witnessed in the last one hour how badly I wanted to win. I mean, there I was: sweating, panting, strategizing! Giving it my one hundred per cent.'

He had finished packing and they had started to walk towards the car-park.

'And it's not only me. Going by the number of people who enjoy their daily sport, a lot of folks seem to be defying Nietzsche. Just that...' he trailed off

'Just that?'

'Just that they're not able to replicate that trick in everyday life.'

Vini didn't reply and they kept walking in silence. Something seemed to be causing her consternation. At length, she meekly enquired, 'Loving things enthusiastically, but not allowing them to matter; do you do it for absolutely everything?'

The dissonance in her tone was palpable; a clear giveaway that she had included herself in the ambit of Raghu's remark. Obviously, this was not an upshot that Raghu had anticipated. He instinctively shot a glance at her. He at once knew that his words would not be easily undone.

'Not everything,' was the protracted reply that finally fell off his lips. It was an instinctive answer and the veracity of the words didn't instantly dawn upon him. But the moment it did, he said aloud those same words once again; this time with deliberation. 'Definitely not everything.' Then, as if to emphasize his words, he slid his arm around her shoulders and gave them an assuring squeeze. The assurance was as much for him as it was for her, but the perceived slenderness of her frame only aggravated his sentiments of helplessness. Impulsively, he tightened his clasp. What followed was a realization about the vainness of attempting to hold on, and that left Raghu with little option but to once again revert to the refuge of words, which, regrettably, were absconding. Briny emotions held them hostage and threatened to drown them if he so much as opened his mouth. And what ultimately came to prevail once again was silence.

With moist eyes, Raghu looked heavenwards. The view happened to be a bit blurred, but this time, there was no ceiling.

www.ingramcontent.com/pod-product-compliance
Lightning Source LLC
Chambersburg PA
CBHW022140060526
44654CB000043B/607